Britain's WATERWAYS
Cruising rings & other things

Contents

Designed, edited and produced by GEOprojects (UK) Limited.
Copyright © Brian Roberts 2001. The right of Brian Roberts to be identified as the author of the text has been asserted by
him in accordance with the Copyright, Design and Patents Act 1988.
Maps based upon Ordnance Survey mapping with the permission of the Controller of Her Majesty's Stationery Office.
© Crown copyright (43372U).

All possible care was taken in the preparation of this book and, whilst the publishers would be grateful to learn of any
errors, they regret they can accept no responsibility for any inaccuracies and for any expense or loss thereby caused.

The representation on the maps of any road, path or open space is no evidence of the existence of a right of way.

Printed in Lebanon.
122

GEOprojects (UK) Ltd.
9-10 Southern Court
South Street
Reading
RG1 4QS

Tel: 0118 939 3567
Fax: 0118 959 8283

GEO projects

Ways of using this book

We hope this book will help to answer some of the queries that occur when you are first inclined to take to the water. The best way the book can help depends on 'where you are coming from'.

How long have you got?
The first five chapters of the book are related to the time you have available for your holiday, ranging from an afternoon to any time in excess of two weeks.

Do you want to start close to home?
Maps in the book cover most of the country. Hirebases are shown alongside the waterways. Seek out somewhere close to your home town.

Where do you want to visit?
Each suggested route includes visitor attractions to be found along the way. Most of them are within a half hour walk of the water, with a few beyond that distance indicated as 'longer walks'.

This is clearly a personal selection and is only scratching the surface of places that could be visited within a short walk of a waterway.

Do you seek the 'Seven Wonders'?
Robert Aickman of the Inland Waterways Association described what he considered the 'Seven Wonders' of the waterways. These are located on the key map opposite.

Hire boats at Trevor, Llangollen Canal

What is the name of your chosen waterway?
Individual canal companies had fiercely individual characters; they were never really team players. The names as given to waterways by their original owners are often still in use today and there is an index of the waterways featured in this book on page 80.

Are you meeting friends for your holiday?
A railway station that serves a large number of towns will be the most convenient target for a group of friends converging from around the country. Some might be sufficiently close to a hirebase to influence your choice of starting point.

What is included.
All route descriptions start with the names of the individual waterways involved, their main engineering features and an estimate of the time needed for the complete route.

Some visitor attractions within a short walk of a boat are suggested plus some waterway features you might find to distract you on your way.

Some possible detours may be suggested. If a short cut is feasible it is indicated. Future waterway projects that might open up other possibilities are also noted.

Key map.
The connected system of England and Wales is shown opposite. Some isolated waterways are described within the book on the pages indicated. Some of the holidays suggested are in the form of a 'ring' of waterways and the appropriate page number is shown at the centre of the ring.

The Broads is an independent network described starting on page 54 and the chapter describing the glorious waterways of Scotland starts on page 58.

All the waterways in the country are shown in the Regional Maps on pages 62 - 75.

SKYE

INVERNESS

 58

ABERDEEN

S C O T L A N D

Neptune's Staircase
FORT WILLIAM

MULL

DUNDEE

PERTH

60
Falkirk
Wheel

EDINBURGH

ISLAY

GLASGOW

ARRAN

ARRAN

DUMFRIES

CARLISLE

NEWCASTLE
UPON TYNE

MIDDLESBROUGH

ISLE OF
MAN

SCARBOROUGH

	Broad navigation
	Narrow navigation
	Waterway under restoration
34	Page number for cruising ring or other route
◆	The Seven Wonders (see page 79)
◇	Other special features

HOLYHEAD

ANGLESEY

Bingley
Five Rise
Locks

YORK

LEEDS

KINGSTON
UPON HULL

16 Burnley
Embankment

50 Tuel Lane
Lock

32 Standedge Tunnel

Barton
Swing
Aqueduct

MANCHESTER

Marple
Aqueduct

SHEFFIELD

LINCOLN

28 Anderton Lift

LIVERPOOL

CHESTER

Harecastle
Tunnels

10 STOKE-ON-TRENT

ENGLAND

Pontcysyllte
Aqueduct

12

40

NOTTINGHAM

The
Wash

KING'S LYNN

NORWICH

54

CARDIGAN
BAY

ABERYSTWYTH

WALES

22

18

Dudley Tunnel

BIRMINGHAM

34

Tardebigge Rocks

30

Leicester
PETERBOROUGH

Foxton
Inclined
Plane

38 Coventry

Lapworth Locks

9   25

WORCESTER

NORTHAMPTON

48

CAMBRIDGE

IPSWICH

Blisworth
Tunnel

20

GLOUCESTER

National
Waterways
Museum

44

6

OXFORD

17

LONDON

SWANSEA

CARDIFF

BRISTOL

14

8

BRISTOL CHANNEL

BATH

Caen
Hill
Locks

36

NEWBURY

READING

24

GUILDFORD

MAIDSTONE

DOVER

CRAWLEY

BRIGHTON

SOUTHAMPTON

ISLE OF
WIGHT

PLYMOUTH

PENZANCE

Scale 1: 2 750 000

0   25   50 miles

0   50   100 kilometres

Frequently Asked Questions

Conversations alongside water often include queries about the boat itself, the holiday, the where, when and how of boating. Part of the pleasure of being on the water is the people you meet and the openness amongst everybody involved. Most people manage a greeting or a wave, even if only from afar.

Questions raised below are typical of those asked by passers by, the gongoozlers, but with some sometimes asked by 'rookie' hirers added. A few, essentially technical queries, are at the end.

General

Where can we visit?

Anywhere within a short walk of towpath.

There are thousands of visitor attractions on or near the 3000 miles of canals and rivers, only some of which can be featured within the pages of this book. Many places within a half hour walk of the towpath have been suggested. There are others beyond that limit which can be reached if you decide to tie up for a day or where you all pile into a taxi or use a local tram for a short diversion 'on the bank'. A few are noted.

After all, the boat has 'en-suite hotel rooms' and can be a base for your visits.

What can we see?

Towpath hedges are refuge for wild flowers and harbour wildlife - **heron**, **voles**, **kingfishers and swans** can all be seen by the sharp-eyed. Rivers and canals pass through **huge swathes of countryside** and offer visits through and near many National Parks and Areas of Outstanding Natural Beauty.

Roman towns such as London, Lincoln, Bath, York and Chester, **seats of learning** such as Oxford and Cambridge, **theatrical centres** such as Stratford and Llangollen are all served by waterways.

The canal network helped cities like **Manchester**, **Birmingham** and **Nottingham** and **the Potteries** to grow during our Industrial Revolution and they are full of **industrial archaeology** - both on their original sites and in living museums. Their canals have survived for over 200 years - you can still get alongside by water.

The waterway system itself is a historical record, made before diesel power and dumper trucks, before electricity and computers, before contour mapping and total stations. The **historical record** includes pioneering **feats of engineering**, designs that would be triple checked today, but in those times were based on field experiments, faith in people and experience of mining. **Construction** contracts involved more men than were mobilized for war, thousands of **bridges and cuttings**, huge, sometimes leaking, **embankments** that drove men to their beds with worry. **Tunnels** bigger than any coal shaft before them, **aqueducts** carrying bigger loads than anything the Romans built for us.

Places like **Little Venice**, **Wigan Pier** and **Castlefield**, and structures such as the **Anderton** Lift, **Foxton** Inclined Plane, **Pontcysyllte** Aqueduct and **Standedge** Tunnel are there to see on the waterways themselves. They can be visited by boat or by road. All can be found on one or more of the maps on the following pages - with short descriptions alongside.

Getting afloat

What type of holiday would you like?

Hotel luxury

There is an increasing number of hotel boats with the luxury of individual cabins, a cuisine of high standard and where everything to do with travelling is done for you (although if you do feel like helping you are welcome). The timetable is given in advance and you join the boat at one place on one weekend and leave it from somewhere else entirely different.

Self drive

Hire boats you work yourself, with the help of your crew. You have to make some choices before you start and this anticipation can be half the fun!

Canoeing

Simplest way to get on water but not designed for

Traditional Boat Rally, Henley-on-Thames

long distances unless you are a specialist. Devizes to Westminster is 125 miles and 77 locks.

Camping skiff

Victorians favoured this adventure. Jerome K Jerome was one of **'Three Men in a Boat'** - not forgetting the dog. A skiff was hired and propelled *down river*, nights being on the skiff under the stars with a canvas roof pulled over some hoops. The skiffs were returned *up river* - by road. It can still be done.

Volunteer

Many canals we use today would not have been 'saved' except for the summer gatherings of able bodied volunteers who undertake restoration work.

Skills are taught, people are introduced, evening relaxation is part of the deal and the authorities are impressed.

Why go by water?

'There is nothing- absolutely nothing - half so much worth doing as simply messing about in boats'. So said Ratty in **'Wind in the Willows'** and it is difficult to disagree. Progress along water is steady, a

rate dictated by the nature of water. It is a different world and wraps its inhabitants in different priorities. Away from the frenetic everyday world your whole body slows down, so much so you often cannot remember what day of the week it is! Some suggest it is 'the fastest way of slowing down'.

How fast?

Your rate of progress as seen by anyone following in a car is VERY slow. But there should be no reason to rush. You are on holiday and at locks it might be necessary to wait your turn anyway. The joy is the smooth glide along the water, not the achievement of rat-race targets. Ultimately your rate of progress depends on how many hours of movement you want to put into the day. After a typical 'holiday start' of say 10am, a two hour break for lunch, perhaps a short walk into town - 4 hours per day of actual travelling may be all that is left!

What else can we plan to do as well?

Allow time to do 'off-cut' activities.

Visit a theme park or your maiden aunt, perhaps see a film. Foraging for provisions among the small specialist butchers, bakers and greengrocers of an unfamiliar town can be an adventure in itself but also requires time. So does window shopping or buying major souvenirs of the trip eg real antiques or modern pottery! But you may not want to plan at all - you are on holiday.

Can we get lost?

Yes, in the sense of being well removed from familiar landmarks and beginning to learn new places in a new landscape.

But in the sense that you will always know your way home - no, you won't be lost!

There are so few ways a boat can go across the country that there are very few junctions involved in the twists and turns of traversing the land. The routes within this book are described using junction names. They are often gloriously memorable.

How long away?
The waterway system today offers a wide choice to the recreational boater - from short breaks mid-week or for a long weekend, to two and three week cruises or even longer. Some hire companies can even arrange for one-way trips between two cooperating bases.

What should we take with us?
Holiday reading, maps, canal and local guide books, camera, bird recognition book, some board games for the evenings, two packs of cards (we play canasta) mobile phone and camcorders! Just remember the cords to a cigarette lighter for your source of 12V.

Cruising rings and other things
There are two very fundamental cruising alternatives - a **'ring'** or **'out and return'**.

'Out and return' makes it easy to concentrate on an area of waterway but always with a choice of being tempted to stop longer, add a detour or deviate from the original ideas. But for some this is a little too hazy. They like to know something of where they will be, for instance so they can arrange for friends to visit. So anticipating the details before you start can be part of the fun.

Decisions, decisions - even on rings. The book assumes you travel clockwise, but one choice may be, at least among the left-handed amongst us, to travel anticlockwise.

Even an 'out and return' journey has the choice of whether to turn left or turn right when leaving the hirebase! You can, of course, plan to do a little of both, which involves returning past the hirebase the day before you are due back and making a short exploration in the 'other' direction. The joy of such a plan is that if you dawdle too much on the main leg you can leave the 'other' direction for another time.

If you like to plan ahead it is useful to have a 'Plan A' and a 'Plan B' for each decision you may take.

The world of waterways does not attempt to offer airline timetable reliability. So you need to make an extra allowance of time for possible changes due to circumstances beyond your control eg closed locks, queues, adverse river flows, the weather forecast.

Easiest of all plans might be called 'Plan C' - just journey along the waterway for roughly half the allotted time, turn round and return - nice and simple - a bit of an adventure as you only discover where you arrive on a 'day-by-day' basis - a distance dependent solely on conditions as found at the time.

If you stagger the start of the return journey by half a day or so then all the lunch and night stops will be in different places to those on the way out.

How soon can we start?
Hiring normally starts after noon as the boat will have come back that morning and it will have been prepared for you in the meantime.

Your party will need to settle in, you will be shown all the facilities on board - central heating, engine, flush toilet, bathroom, kitchen - and any novices will learn the basics of 'driving' the boat. Your questions will be answered.

Allow for a first cup of tea and you might plan up

to two hours travelling on the first day before mooring for the night - alongside a nearby waterside hostelry perhaps - ask the hirebase staff.

Technical

Do I need a licence?
You do not need a special licence to drive a boat. The hirebase will 'show you the ropes' before you set off and slow progress in an all steel vehicle means there is little damage you can do to the boat itself, although the paintwork might be vulnerable.

Some firms run 'Trial days' where you can spend an afternoon getting advice and a little practice. There is usually a fee, but this is knocked off the cost of boat hire if you make a holiday booking.

What is a flight of locks?
A bit like a flight of stairs which has a series of steps one after another, a flight of locks has a series of locks one after another. Staircase locks, however, are a bit more complicated. Essentially staircase locks are so close together that the top gates of one are the same piece of wood as the bottom gates of the next.

Who operates the locks?
On rivers such as the Severn and the Thames it is done for you! On canals it is a case of 'Do-It-Yourself' with waterways staff assisting at major flights of locks. D-I-Y lock operation is easily accomplished by any semi-fit person. Youngsters soon get the idea and have been known to take over and do all the work. Ensure they take care.

Can everybody do everything?
Yes, then everybody gets to know what is involved in steering, working locks, cooking (!) etc. and it's more fun too. Some experienced crews get to specialise, but that comes later.

What is a winding hole?
It is a wider piece of canal where boats can perform the equivalent of a three point turn in order to go back the way they came. An indentation in the bank allows the bows of a narrowboat to be held whilst the prevailing wind blows the boat round. Hence the unusual pronunciation - '**wind**ing hole'.

Do you tie up or moor?
Both. This book uses 'tie up' to indicate a temporary stop and 'mooring' for longer - eg overnight.

When moored, experienced boaters often add 'springer ropes' - additional longer ropes to create a firm triangle which can stop the boat riding fore and aft when other boats pass - especially on busy narrow canals. On rivers all ropes have to be a little slack as there is a chance that levels may change overnight.

Why are engines stronger than the speed limit allows?
Boats use both canal waters and the waters of rivers. Speed limit for canals is 4 mph and on rivers it is often the same. However, water in rivers can flow downstream at a cracking pace, often faster than 4 mph. A boat pushing upstream at 4 mph against this moving water would appear to remain stationary and not move, except perhaps backwards!

Therefore boat engines are strong and are capable of propelling along the still waters of canals much

Hotel Boat Pair

faster than the speed limit. This is designed for safety on rivers, not an invitation to break the speed limit on canals, imposed because a heavy wash behind a speeding boat can damage 200 year old canal banks and can lead to leaks.

How do you tackle overtaking?
Generally, you don't. Canals are too narrow, another boat may be coming the other way, emerging from around the next corner or through the next bridge-hole. If you are content to be slower than average and you accumulate 3 or 4 boats in a queue behind, just kill your speed, pull over to the towpath, tie up for 5 minutes, let them pass and you will soon have the joy of independence again.

If it is busy and there are locks ahead you may, of course, choose to keep your place in the queue.

Should I buy a boat?
Maybe, eventually! Customers of boat-builders generally have already hired two or more boats before they place their orders, partly to test different saloon / bedroom arrangements, partly to test the differences between canal and river conditions.

In many ways hiring is better than owning. Owners have to start each trip from exactly the place they finished their last one. Hirers have the option of starting each trip from points that are dozens, even hundreds, of miles apart.

How much?
Boats are expensive to buy - they are generally the cost of two BMWs. Hiring prices, on the basis of per person per day for up to six on a boat, depend on the standard of the boat (some are of extremely high quality), whether you are going in high or low season, whether it is for a short break or longer.

A week's holiday in July 2001 varied between £17 and £34 per person per night.

What is a 'gongoozler'?
The boaters affectionate name for the **walkers** and **onlookers** who often crowd together along the towpaths to follow, sometimes critically, the progress of boats, especially as they pass through the locks.

One Afternoon

The best way to know if you might enjoy a holiday on water is to give it a try. Punting on the shallow rivers of Cambridge or Oxford is a difficult skill to acquire in an afternoon and, although it is a fun way to start, hiring rowing boats and canoes on the local park lake is not really a preparation for the wider and deeper waters of our rivers and canals. Most trips confined to an afternoon involve a short run away from the base, a visit to a local attraction and eventual return. This is how most of the possible taster trips noted below are arranged.

However, Oxford is one place on the waterway system where two waterways are connected twice within a very short distance, thus allowing a 'ring' cruise in one afternoon.

Taster trips

Join a group, or potter yourself.

To get a taste of travelling on water in a larger boat there are **restaurant boats** or **evening discos** giving trips in places as far apart as London and York.

There are **tourist waterbuses** along canals in Wigan, Birmingham and many other parts of the country. Many **ferries** cross river estuaries such as Dartmouth. If you live near Woolwich, east of London, the ferry across the Thames is free of charge.

There are **charitable groups** who have had special 'Community Boats'constructed with the needs of special groups and the disabled in mind. These have lifts and ramps for wheelchair users and special arrangements for steering from a seated position. Their trips are cheap and sometimes free.

There are over fifty **waterway societies** who are promoting the restoration of abandoned or derelict canals. Some of these are able to run trip boats on those isolated parts of the alignment that they have managed to restore to water. The Inland Waterways Association (Tel: 01923 711114) will probably guide you to your nearest.

There are also quite a few **'boat gatherings'**, **'boat shows'** or **'canal days'** around the country. Two of the oldest are probably the 'Canalway Cavalcade' at Little Venice, London on the early May Bank Holiday and the Boat Show in the Midlands, now at Crick, every late May Bank Holiday. These often have cheap or even free **boat trips** as part of their attractions.

Many of the hirebases listed in the appendix have smaller **'day boats'** that have a cabin, dining table and kitchen but no sleeping arrangements. They can be reserved for a private afternoon trip to the local picnic site or hostelry.

I suppose the ultimate trial is a **one night stand**, mid afternoon to mid morning, but only some boatyards offer this. To be honest - on a per person per night basis - this is an unsatisfactory and expensive way of doing it. You have only just settled in when it is time to leave and the hirebase has to bear the costs of preparing the boat for the next group. Much better to try for **a long weekend**.

Most boatyards welcome inspection by prospective customers and many make formal arrangements to take people out on the water to show off their boats.

Some have **'open days'** where you can try your hand, some even arrange **'familiarisation days'** which, for a small fee, involve a long afternoon on a boat learning the ropes and trying the manoeuvres. The fee is usually returned when booking a holiday with the same hirebase.

Almost every hirebase on the system will encourage a trial trip. See complete hirebase listing on pages 76 - 78.

Oxford Ring

Short ring and three longer detours.

River Thames
Four Ways Jcn - Fiddler's Island - Port Meadow - Godstow Lock - King's Lock
Duke's Cut (1789)
King's Lock - Duke's Cut Lock
Oxford Canal (1790)
Duke's Cut - Wolvercote - Isis Lock

Allow 3 hours travelling.
3 miles of canal, 3 miles of river, 3 narrow locks,
2 river locks operated by lock keepers.

A tour around Port Meadow, an ancient low lying summer grazing, overwashed during winter.

This ring has everything - friendly lock keepers, DIY canal locks, tight meanders and wide reaches of river, tree lined straight-but-still length of canal, city centre waterway junction, bustling boatyard, back gardens with rowboats, an Agenda 21 boating community and immaculate college playing fields. Four handy hostelries - two on the river, an 800 year old thatched pub and a former Abbey hospice - and two on the canal at bridges 236 and 240.

Visitor attractions

Godstow Abbey Ruins (1138-1646)
Nunnery, formerly site of pilgrimage to tomb of Henry II's mistress Rosamond the Fair, poisoned by Queen Eleanor (1177). The river crossing, domestic buildings and hospice survived Cromwell's Fairfax attacks. Hospice is now the 'Trout Inn'.
Tie up near Godstow Bridge.
Port Meadow
Freemen of Oxford were given the grazing rights for cattle and horses by King Alfred when he founded the City. They are jealously guarded and still exercised to this day. Contains Bronze Age burials, Port Meadow special geese (hybrid of wild and domestic varieties) and on the lowest lying - and never ploughed - area near Medley, a Site of Special Scientific Interest (SSSI), with sweet floating grass

and water mint.
To explore on foot, tie up near Bossoms Boatyard. Go east across Medley Footbridge to the Meadow.
Ashmolean Museum (Tel: 01865 278000)
Elias Ashmole gave his collection to the University (1683) to form the basis of the oldest public museum in England. Fine Art, archeology. Recently refurbished.
Tie up near Isis Lock. Walk past Hythe Bridge.
St George's Tower: Oxford Castle
First building within castle walls. Church where first scholars of Oxford were taught was sealed later. Dominates site of Norman mill (demolished 1935).
Tie up near Isis Lock. Walk to Hythe Bridge, cross and follow Castle Mill Stream to Quaking Bridge.
Oxford Story (Tel: 01865 790055)
One hour introduction to all that is Oxford University. Sit in a replica of a medieval scholar's desk and journey from the 1200s when learning began.
Tie up near Isis Lock. Walk past Hythe Bridge, cross into George Street, at the end enter Broad Street.
Museum of Modern Art
Small gallery with international reputation, tucked away in narrow Pembroke Street near Littlegate.
Tie up near Folly Bridge and walk up St Aldates.
Bodleian Library (Tel: 01865 277000)
Major depository of learning, receives a copy of all UK publications. So respected by Oliver Cromwell that he posted guards to forbid entry to marauding soldiers after taking Oxford (Civil War 1646).
Tie up near Isis Lock. Walk past Hythe Bridge, cross into George Street, at the end enter Broad Street.
St Martin's Tower, Carfax (1032)
Overlooking the cross roads at the centre of the walled city, where fresh water was delivered from out of town by conduit. A climb to the top of the tower (small fee) is well rewarded with an overview of the

plains of the two rivers, Thames and Cherwell, and the city that grew between them.

Tie up near Isis Lock. Walk past Hythe Bridge, turn right up New Road into Queen Street pedestrian area.

Oxford Colleges
Stone built quadrangles with porters' lodges at the gates. In term time visitors are allowed in the afternoons, in vacations, longer. Accredited guides gain controlled access. Tranquillity inside, city life outside. There is no University as such, but 35 independent colleges and halls provide the teaching.

Tie up near Isis Lock. Walk past Hythe Bridge. Nuffield College and Worcester College are first.

Oxford Castle Mound (1071)
Ancient remains of Royalist Castle (1651).

Visit by appointment with Museum of Oxford. Tie up near Isis Lock. Walk past Hythe Bridge into New Road (1776).

Binsey Treacle Well
According to Alice's guide in wonderland this well had a supply of treacle at the bottom. The 'Perch' has swings, slides and climbing frames for present day kids and more normal refreshments for adults.

Tie up on landing stage and walk a few yards inland.

Aristotle Lane Recreation Ground
Swings, slides and kick-about grass next to the canal.

Tie up south of Bridge 240. To find Port Meadow go via a pedestrian lane westwards and over a railway.

Waterway distractions

Duke's Cut Lock (1789)
Built before levels on upper River Thames were controlled by weirs and locks, this lock had to cope with a wide variation of water levels. Sometimes the canal was higher than the river, at other times the river was in flood and higher than the canal. Thus gates on the original lock had to 'face both ways'. Recesses for a third set of gates can still be seen.

Look carefully when passing through the lock.

Isis Lock (1796)
Made by inmates of Oxford Gaol to connect the canal with the River Thames. Built to full width to allow river barges access to the warehouses around the canal terminal basin but later 'narrowed' as too much water moved from canal to river with each boat passing. Delightful setting with water on every side and a Horseley Iron Works towpath bridge.

Tie up near the lock itself.

Hythe Bridge Street Basin
A temporary car park for many years, this site, together with the coal wharf beyond Worcester Street, was sold (1936) to Lord Nuffield who then endowed Nuffield College with them both. The College has developed around the site of the Coal Arm, echoed by the shape of the fish pond within the grounds. The main basin site is surrounded by roads carrying double-decker buses and may no longer be entirely suitable for college purposes.

Look over the parapet of Hythe Bridge.

London, Midland and Scottish Railway Bridge
Low level swing bridge must open for water traffic. Waiting is required for a 'window of opportunity'.

Always open. See undergrowth by Sheepwash channel.

Thames Lock Keepers
At every one of 43 locks on the non-tidal Thames. Helpful, good humoured controllers of boats of every kind. Packing them in - steel first, GRP afterwards. In slack periods will ring ahead to warn the next lock

Visitor moorings, Oxford from Isis Lock

you are coming. They could have it ready for you.

King's Lock and Godstow Lock on this ring.

Worth a detour

Christ Church Meadows
Head of the River Course runs from Iffley and finishes in front of Christ Church Meadows. Scene of much celebration during Eights Week (end of May). The Meadow, given to support a chantry in the old Priory of St Frideswide, is still grazed by cattle and parts are open to the public. Much used by relaxing tourists in summer.

Tie up downstream of Folly Bridge.

University Boathouses
Built as replacement for elaborate College Barges which were moored near here and succumbed to fire.

Tie up near Folly Bridge. Seen from the towpath.

Botanical Gardens (1621)
Earliest in Britain. Set up to study the medicinal value of meadowlands flora, enlarged to include imported plants. Source of the escaped Sicilian plant - Oxford Ragwort - now considered a weed.

Tie up downstream of Folly Bridge.

Magdalen Bridge
Closed on May Day - for the assembled crowds to hear the dawn chorus of Magdalen College Choir singing from the top of the Tower. Centre for hiring punts at other times.

Tie up near Folly Bridge. Walk downstream along the north bank and up past the Botanical Gardens.

Angel and Greyhound Meadow
The River Cherwell passes by one of many open areas covered with revising students on warm spring days.

Tie up near Folly Bridge. Walk downstream along the north bank and up past the Botanical Gardens.

St Mary's Church, Iffley
Classic Norman Romanesque style from 1100s. Four square towers and rich carving inside and out.

Tie up near Iffley Lock. Cross the lock gates, past the chamber of the early pound lock and up the hill.

Worth a longer detour

Round House, Lechlade
Thames and Severn Canal lock keepers' house and effective limit of navigation for powered craft. Unspoilt rural reaches of the River Thames. Kelmscott Manor, Radcot Bridge, Newbridge, Bablock Hythe, Swinford Toll Bridge and Wytham Great Wood.

26 miles, 9 locks each way. Allow 17 hours.

St Helen's Wharf, Abingdon
South on the Thames, past the sites of three of the oldest locks in the country - at Iffley, at Sandford (now rebuilt) and on Swift Ditch (1635). Former County Town of Berkshire. Abbey ruins. county hall. Glorious boater-friendly moorings.

9 miles, 3 locks each way. Allow 6 hours.

Thrupp
Canal village. Stone cottages overlooking the canal. Popular pubs. Gunpowder wharf. Thrupp Wide.

4½ miles, 2 locks each way. Allow 3 hours.

Future Possibilities
Reinstatement of the former Oxford Canal Terminal Basin at Hythe Bridge Street may be complete one day. Thus creating 48 hour visitor moorings in the heart of Oxford City which will be more than a match for those currently found at Bath and Stratford-upon-Avon.

ℹ️ Tourist Information
Oxford Tel: 01865 726871

GEO Cruising Maps
GEOprojects: *Oxford Canal*
GEOprojects: *Thames, the river and the path*

Start Points
15	Anlgo Welsh Waterway Holidays	58	College Cruisers
15	Oxfordshire Narrowboats	82	Kingcraft
26	Avalon Narrowboat Co	91	Cotswold Boat Hire
		97	Red Line Cruisers

East London Ring

Long Weekend

Friday afternoon to Monday morning is a weekend which provides three nights on the water. Other short breaks on offer at many bases are the four night midweek break from Monday afternoon to Friday morning. In both cases this is long enough to lose your sense of time and that is one of the joys of a holiday on water - you can get to the stage that you do not know what day of the week it is.

Choices of where to go in such a short break are fairly limited from any one hirebase. Basically you can turn right or left out of the marina, journey for day, spend a day at ease and spend the last day on the return journey. But this does not mean you have no choice. Some hirebaes are in the cities, some near the countryside. Where you travel depends only on where you choose to start and there is a huge variety of possible start points which are all shown on the maps.

Hirebases that are close to rail stations allow friends to meet from different points of the compass without the distracting hassle of driving either side of the short holiday.

The two suggestions made here are, unusually, in the form of small rings. Droitwich will only be operational when some current restoration works are complete but it allows me to note the differing kinds of waterway experiences that are available and when it is fully open it will provide a perfect introduction to many facets of boating on Britain's Waterways.

Three Mills Visitor Centre

East London Ring

Two parks, Three Mills and a basin.

Hertford Union Canal (1838)
Hertford Union Jcn - Victoria Park - Old Ford Jcn
Lee Navigation (1769)
Old Ford - Three Mills - Bow Locks
Limehouse Cut (1770, 1968)
Bow Locks - Limehouse Basin
Regent's Canal (1820)
Limehouse Basin - Mile End - Hertford Union Jcn

Allow 4 hours travelling on the ring itself plus 9½ hours from hirebase to ring.
6 miles of wide canal, 8 wide locks.

A tiny ring lined with attractions open at weekends provides a gentle target from the nearest hirebases.

Visitor attractions
Bow Wharf
Quayside fun, redeveloped from former glue factory warehouses, Jongleurs Comedy Club, real ale and other bars. (Jongleurs Tel: 020 7564 2500).
Tie up near Hertford Union Junction.
Victoria Park
Major green lung developed in Queen Victoria's days

follows the canal for almost a mile.
Tie up at Three Colt Bridge.
Three Mills Visitor Centre (Tel: 020 8983 1121)
Early (1776) environmentally sound energy source. Incoming tides are held back in a 50 acre lake and then released under waterwheels to produce over 150 horsepower driving eight pairs of millstones.
Tie up next to the mills. Open Sunday afternoons.
Dr Barnardo's Ragged School
Museum showing East London conditions of poverty and charitable moves to improve education in late 1800s. Lord Shaftesbury assisted.
Tie up near Johnson's Lock, No 10.

Waterway distractions
Sir George Duckett's Cut (1830)
Sir George, owner of Stort Navigation, paid for this short canal with three wide locks but he set toll charges too high and it failed. Sold to Regent's Canal.
Now known as the Hertford Union Canal.
Bow Back Rivers
Complex of tidal creeks and canalised water at the mouth of River Lee as it discharges into the Thames. Now protected by a flood barrier on Bow Creek.
Tie up near Old Ford Lock. Walk the towpaths.
Limehouse Basin
Barges and narrowboats crowded the basin to offload direct over the side from seagoing ships. Now a

Tower Bridge, London

haven for all kinds of boats - masted seagoing yachts and wide beam barges.
Tie up in the basin.

ℹ️ *Tourist Information*
London Tourist Board
Tel: 09068 663344 *(Premium rate line)*
Website: www.londontouristboard.com

GEO *Cruising Maps*
GEOprojects: *Lee and Stort Navigations with the East London Ring*
GEOprojects: *Grand Union Canal map 3, Fenny Stratford to the Thames*

Start Points
2 Adelaide Marine

2 London & Home Counties Narrowboat Holidays

Droitwich Ring
Short but everything on offer, eventually.

Worcester and Birmingham Canal (1815)
  Hanbury Wharf -Dunhampstead - Offerton -
  Bilford - Commandery - Diglis Basins
River Severn Navigation (1804 towpath)
  Diglis Basins - Sabrina - Bevere - Hawford Jcn
Droitwich (Barge) Canal (1771, 1806-1939, 200?)
  Hawford Jcn - Ladywood - Swing bridges - Vines
  Park
Droitwich Junction Canal (1854-1939, 200?)
  Vines Park - Seven locks - Hanbury Wharf

*When the restoration is complete this will be the only
short journey that includes a narrow canal with D-I-Y
locks, a lively river with a manned lock and wide
locks on a wide canal.*

*Allow 14 hours travelling on the ring.
10 miles of narrow canal, 3 miles of lively river, 9
miles of wide canal, 1 tunnel, 21 narrow locks, 8
wide locks, 1 huge manned river lock. Total of 22
miles with 30 locks.*

Lots of locks, mostly on the narrow Worcester &
Birmingham Canal but the huge one on the River
Severn is under the control of a lock keeper. A
short tunnel, upstream river travel, early (barge)
canal with wide locks by Brindley, Droitwich Spa
and Worcester to visit, all this could take longer
than a weekend. As a summer trial of boating
experiences in a short time this will not be
bettered. Much of the towpath is already open.

Visitor attractions
Worcester
Faithful City, Civil War Rooms, Fine Porcelain,
Brown Sauce. Cathedral with King John (1216) set in
marvellous close overlooking the river.
*Man-powered ferry across Severn, summer weekends.
Tie up upstream of Worcester Road Bridge.*
Droitwich Spa
A Roman 'wich' defended by a fort (AD60), supplier

Worcester Cathedral from the River Severn

of salt till 1922. Spa rooms with salt baths, believed
to be beneficial after general cholera epidemic (1832).
*Isolated navigation. Needs one blockage removed.
Junction Canal currently under restoration (2001).*
Chateau Impney (1875)
Entrepreneur, benefactor and son of a bargeowner,
John Corbett built this home for his wife Anna and
their five children in the grand 'Versailles' style from
the profits of a 'new salt source' at Stoke Prior (1828).
Tie up on Junction Canal. Follow the footpath north.

Waterway distractions
Hanbury Wharf
Crossed by the ancient straight Roman 'Salt Way'
this wharf was the first pound of the Droitwich
Junction Canal (narrow), built too late to stem the
loss of salt trade to the new-fangled railways.
*Tie up near Bridge 34. Walk the Junction Canal
towpath. See the latest achievements of the Waterway
Recovery Group volunteers - restored locks awaiting
water.*
Dunhampstead Tunnel
Shortest tunnel on this canal, only 690 feet long with
a handrail to pull boats along. Horsepath over the top.
Tie up at Bridge 30.
Diglis Basins
Two basins served from the variable river by very
wide (18'6") locks. Renovation project under way.
Tie up on towpath short of the Basins themselves.
Bevere Lock and weir (Tel: 01905 640275)
Wooded setting, refuge for people fleeing troubles in
Worcester. Lock keeper's famous flower displays.
Tie up and follow instructions.
Salwarpe Valley at Hawford
This Saxon 'salty boathaul' provides the route for the
Barge Canal and supports unique salt-tolerant plant
life. Underground water is also salty and created an
excellent 'earth' terminal for British Broadcasting
Corporation's long wave transmitter (1934).
*Only light craft can use the boatyard just upstream
from the Severn. Currently (2001) the A449 makes a
turn into the Barge Canal at Hawford rather
pointless.*
Porter's Mill (1881)
One of seven watermills along the River Salwarpe
noted in the Domesday Book (1086). Now a private
residence.
*Tie up near Lock 5 on the Barge Canal. Walk to the
river. Photogenic.*
Vines Park, Droitwich Spa
Reclaimed salt workings. Early swing bridges
balanced on ancient roller bearings. Modern marina
and local trip boat.
*Limit of navigation for the Barge Canal. End to end
connection with the narrow Junction Canal which
will be restored using River Salwarpe's channel to a
Body Brook culvert under M5. Waterway Recovery
Group are finishing old Locks 1-3, and new Locks 4-7
will be needed. Total restoration costs are estimated
at £7.6 million.*

Worth a detour
Stourport Basins
Push upstream to early inland port with four basins.
10 miles, 2 river locks. Allow 8 hours travelling.
Upton upon Severn
Run downstream to head off overland for Great
Malvern and the Malvern Hills.
10 miles, 1 river lock. Allow 6 hours travelling.

📖 **Suggested Guide Book**
Jon Axe *Droitwich Spa's Canal* Droitwich Canals
Trust, 2000

ℹ️ **Tourist Information**
Worcester Tel: 01905 726311
Droitwich Spa Tel: 01905 774312

🗺️ **Cruising Maps**
GEOprojects: *Staffordshire and Worcestershire Canal
with the River Severn and the Gloucester and
Sharpness Canal*
GEOprojects: *Worcester and Birmingham Canal with
the Droitwich Canals*

Start Points
[18] Anglo Welsh
  Waterway Holidays
[36] Black Prince Holidays
[44] Brook Line Narrowboat
  Holidays
[109] Starline Narrowboats
[110] Stroudwater Cruisers
[115] Telstar Cruisers Ltd
[122] Viking Afloat

One Week

When travelling for a week away it is most likely that you will move away from the start point for, say, three days and then return along the same water.

The important choice is what you want to see on the way. The surrounding landscape can be urban areas seen from a different viewpoint or countryside, some of which may be classified as an Area of Outstanding Natural Beauty or as a National Park. You can experience a river with lock keeper's assistance or go on a canal where you work the locks yourself. Depending how energetic you feel, you can choose canal routes with few locks or many and if you are claustrophobic you can choose routes without tunnels (or determine to walk over the top) or if you are agrophobic you may need to avoid tall aqueducts.

Some hire companies offer 'one-way, one-week' trips as a collaboration between two hirebases. You park your vehicle at the destination base and then the company transports you and your baggage to the starting point. This is increasingly popular but may be disconcerting to some as you only know the direction you will travel when it is clear which end your boat is starting from.

The suggestions that follow are generally longer branches off the main network, too long to be a detour from other trips, but just enough to allow a fulfilling 'out and return' trip in a week. Also included are two locations where it is feasible to undertake a circular route or ring. This requires a commitment to a timetable as the hirebase expects to welcome you back at the time agreed and the extra dimension this adds to the holiday is not for everyone. It limits the opportunities to stop off at visitor attractions along the way or just to stop to read a book in the sunshine.

If start days of Friday, Saturday or Sunday are available this allows for some relief from the congestion that can occur around the larger hirebases on 'changeover days'.

Caldon Canal
Rural valley close to the Potteries.

Trent and Mersey Canal (1775)
Etruria Jcn
Caldon Canal (1779-1961, 1974)
Etruria Jcn - Stockton Brook Locks - Hazelhurst Jcn - Cheddleton Locks - Froghall Tunnel - Froghall Wharf - Tramroad to limestone quarries
Leek Branch (1802-1944, 1974)
Hazelhurst Jcn - Leek Tunnel - Leek Terminus - Rudyard feeder

Allow 10 hours travelling out and 10 hours back. 25 miles of narrow canal, 1½ miles river, 2 tunnels, 1 aqueduct, 3 lift bridges and 17 narrow locks.

A pair of cul-de-sac waterways which are strictly branches of the Trent and Mersey Canal, they climb up away from the Potteries and down into the tranquil Churnet Valley as it runs through steep gorges down past the Peak District towards Alton and Uttoxeter. A section at the Froghall end was repaired as a narrow concrete channel and requires courtesy and understanding when in use by boaters.

Lush nature has completely reclaimed this area from its very early industrial activity. Hidden in the undergrowth are ironstone quarries, old lime kilns, old coal shafts, flint grinding mills, forges, silk mills, paper mills, watermills, lead smelting, brass casting, brewing:- the only survivors of this vast array of industries are the extraction of 1000 tons a day of silica sand at Oakmoor and the manufacture of copper cabling at Froghall.

Creator of this delightful valley and tributary of the River Dove, the Churnet is a countryman's idyll, fills up after rain and provides a 1½ mile link for the navigation (Oak Meadow Lock to Consall Forge weir).

Visitor attractions
Etruria Hall (1780)
Home of Josiah Wedgwood, inventor and man of vision. Father of the Trent and Mersey Canal.

Now preserved as part of the Moat House Hotel. Nearby factory was transferred to Barlaston in 1940.
Tie up near the Festival Basin. Opposite are the remains of bottle kilns of his 1796 canalside factory.
Etruria Bone and Flint Mill
Now part of the modern Etruria Industrial Museum, Jesse Shirley's Bone and Flint Mill (1857-1972) had 12 grinding pans each driven through sets of gears from a single beam steam engine 'Princess'(1822).

Flints and bones were brought by canal and product sent all over the Potteries. Engine regularly in steam.
Tie up in the wide basin before the new entrance.
Hanley Park
Glorious Victorian park with two ornate footbridges over the canal as it passes through.
Tie up within the park.
Factory Tours and shops (Tel: 01782 319232)
Factories of Royal Doulton at Burslem and Spode at Stoke plus Gladstone Working Pottery Museum at Longton all provide some hands-on experience of creative use of clay and the potter's wheel. A 'China Link Bus' connects these and other attractions.
Tie up near Bridge 8. The Bridgewater Factory shop is canalside. Walk north to Hanley Bus Station.
Brindley Mill and Museum (Tel: 01538 384195)
Brindley died wealthy but prematurely (aged 56) after he caught a chill surveying the Caldon (1772). The Museum displays his notebook and theodolite and includes an early corn mill that he equipped as a young man when he set up in Leek as a millwright (1742) - and it is still working.
Tie up at Bridge 8. Walk to Leek, turn left onto A523. Short walk down to River Churnet.
Deep Hayes Country Park
Includes woods, meadows and pools bequeathed from the industrial past. Reservoir for an iron smelter, ponds from clay workings. Visitor Centre summer weekends.
Canalside near Bridge 39.
Staffordshire Way (1983)
92 mile waymarked walk from Mow Cop to Kinver Edge uses canal towpaths for some of its route.
On the Caldon Canal from Horse Bridge 39 to Cherry Eye Bridge 53. Also on the Staffordshire and Worcestershire Canal and the Trent and Mersey Canal.
Cheddleton Flint Mill (Restored 1969)
Set in the Churnet Valley Gorge, a matching pair of waterwheels used to grind flint for the Potteries.
Tie up alongside. Fellows, Morton & Clayton butty 'Vienna' has been restored and is moored here.
Churnet Valley Railway: Cheddleton Station
North Staffordshire Railway (1978) Ltd is run by volunteers who saved this station building from destruction and renovated it as well as 3 steam locomotives. 6 miles of track have been restored and train rides are available to Froghall and beyond (Tel: 01538 360522).
Tie up near Bridge 44.

Steam Railway and Caldon Canal at Consall Forge

The Flint Mill at Cheddleton

Consall Nature Park and Wild Life Sanctuary

Site of Special Scientific Interest is at the heart of a large nature conservation area (1989). Displays of the dramatic past of the valley and present nature interest are in a Visitor Centre (Tel: 01782 550939).
Easy access from the water (Bridge 50), remote access from the road system.

Knypersley Reservoir

At centre of 114 acre Greenway Bank Country Park. Quiet woodlands, lawns, shrubberies. Gawtons Well.
Tie up near Bridge 28. Longer walk through Endon and Hodgefield towards the head of the River Trent.

Devil's Staircase

Footpath and 100 steps leading to magnificent views over the whole valley.
Tie up near the Black Lion at footbridge 49.

Froghall Wharf

Waymarked walks and a picnic area surrounded by huge reminders of the industrial past. Interpretation boards tell of the cable railway and early plateway that both brought the limestone from higher up.

Restored lime kilns appear like a cliff behind the Wharf House and Stables. Horse-drawn trip boat.
Tie up short of Froghall Tunnel, that is unless you are less than the low (4'9") tunnel headroom.

Alton Towers

Alongside the Churnet, grounds of a stately home turned into the most popular theme park in England.
Tie up near Froghall Wharf and take a taxi, or gird your loins for a long (5 mile) walk up the valley. Starting from Cherry Eye Bridge 53 follow the waymarked 'Staffordshire Way' as far as Lord's Bridge and then the public footpath to Alton Towers.

Waterway distractions

Bedford Staircase Locks

First boaters challenge is to work steadily through this pair of locks rising 19 feet.

Tie up and read the instructions!

Endon Basin

Remains of a railway / canal interchange. Now used as boater's base.
Tie up near Bridge 27.

Hazelhurst Junction and Aqueduct

Created when the Leek Branch fed water into the summit level, a sort of slip road and flyover of canals, includes three locks on the main line.
Tie up at Bridge 35. Walk the figure of eight towpaths.

Leek Branch (1802)

Limestone trade from Froghall and the Caldon Low Quarries was so good that extra water was required. This short branch collected trade from Brindley's town through a short tunnel (now closed) but the main purpose was to create a feeder channel from Rudyard Reservoir, still essential.
Turn off at Hazelhurst Junction.

Rudyard Reservoir

Woods, chalets and sailing. Great views. Created to collect water for the whole Trent and Mersey Canal.
Tie up at Bridge 9. Follow a footpath and cross A53. 'Staffordshire Way' points the way. Almost 3 miles.

Froghall Tunnel

Low headroom tunnel (4'8") 228 feet long. You can see the end, but don't try unless you are sure.
Tie up short - it is not far to walk.

Worth a detour

Harecastle Tunnel and Bosley Locks

North on the Trent and Mersey Canal to the Harecastle Tunnel. The original long narrow tunnel was the boldest engineering of its day and set the dimensions for all future narrowboats. Continue onto the Macclesfield to Bosley Locks. An almost lock-free trip.
16 miles, 1 lock, 1 tunnel. Allow for a wait at the tunnel each way plus 9 hours travelling.

Wedgwood Museum, Bridge 104, Barlaston

South on the Trent and Mersey Canal, within walking distance of the modern factory.
5 miles, 6 locks. Allow 6 hours travelling.

Future possibilities

Two schemes are in the very early stages. One to go north towards the Macclesfield Canal via an enlarged feeder to Rudyard. The other to go south closely following the line of the 1845 railway which itself was built on top of the original canal line to Uttoxeter (1811-1847).

📖 Suggested Guide Book

The Caldon Canal Society: *Guide to The Caldon Canal 2000/1*

ℹ️ Tourist Information

Stoke-on-Trent Tel: 01782 284600
Leek Tel: 01583 381000

🗺️ Cruising Maps

GEOprojects: *Trent and Mersey Canal map 1, Preston Brook to Fradley Junction*
GEOprojects: *Macclesfield and Peak Forest Canals with the Ashton Canal*

Start Points

10 Andersen Boats	51 Canal Cruising
10 Middlewich Narrowboats	Company Ltd
35 Black Prince Holidays	77 Heritage Narrowboats

Llangollen and Montgomery Canals

Two canals in the Welsh mountains.

Ellesmere Canal - Hurleston Branch (1805)
Hurleston Jcn - Wrenbury - Grindley Brook -
Whitchurch - Prees - Ellesmere - Frankton Jcn
Ellesmere Canal - Main Line (1805)
Frankton Jcn - Chirk - Pontcysyllte - Trevor
Navigable feeder (1808)
Trevor - Llangollen - Horseshoe Falls
Ellesmere Canal - Llanymynech Branch (1796)
Frankton Jcn - Queen's Head - Aston Locks
Montgomeryshire Canal (1797)
Guilsfield - Pool Quay - Welshpool - Berriew

Almost 15,000 boats a year take this best known of
all possible cruises, an 'out and return' route
which climbs away from the Cheshire Plain past
rolling fields, across a peat bog and into Wales,
becoming more scenic and clinging ever more
precariously to the mountains as it goes.

Its crowning glory of two tunnels and two
aqueducts all set within steep sided valleys, plus
the 1½ mile walk to Telford's elegant dam across
the River Dee is difficult to surpass in any other
part of the waterway system.

Visitor attractions

Horseshoe Falls
Telford's elegant curving weir across the River Dee
in the mountains. Diverting water to the canal and
supplying Nantwich and beyond at a rate of twelve
million gallons every day.
*Tie up in Llangollen. Walk the feeder channel to
Llantysilio, or ride the Llangollen Steam Railway.*
Llangollen
Valle Crucis Cistercian Monastery, Dinas Bran Castle
- home to King Arthur's knights and family. Every
July home to some of the best musicians in the world
competing in the International Musical Eisteddfod.
Tie up near Siambra-Wen Bridge.
Chirk Castle (Tel: 01691 777701)
Marcher castle of Edward I (1310). Roger Mortimer's
family apartments, state rooms, dungeons, servants'
quarters and gardens with a house for hawks.
*Tie up at north end of Chirk Tunnel, cross over the
canal, walk up to the gates ahead.*

*Allow 18 hours travelling the length from Hurleston
Junction to Llangollen, adding the return journey
gives a total of 36 hours.
45 miles of canal end to end, 3 tunnels, 2 aqueducts,
21 narrow locks, 3 staircase locks, 10 lift bridges.
Seven Wonder: Pontcysyllte Aqueduct*

Canoe, Pontcysyllte

Shropshire's Lake District

Meres that gave their name to Ellesmere, Cole Mere, Blake Mere, White Mere, Newton Mere and simply The Mere. Welcoming to birdlife.
Tie up at the tall Scots pines alongside Cole Mere.
Tie up alongside Blake Mere west of Bridge 56.
Go into Ellesmere Branch. Walk to 'The Mere'.

Whixall Moss

Bog created by the retreating ice cap 10,000 years ago. Difficult for engineers but home to rare insects and plants. Now a Site of Special Scientific Interest.
Tie up near Bridge 45. See the interpretation boards.

Waterway distractions

Pontcysyllte Aqueduct (1007 feet, 126 feet high)

The drama of passing over this monument to early engineering is down to the fact that the iron trough which holds the water is bounded on one side by the towing path with its handrail and on the other by very little at all. Persons of a nervous disposition should remain inside and children be carefully looked after. Horse-drawn and other trip-boats cross the aqueduct.
Tie up in Trevor. Walk across if you care to.

Two Tunnels

Chirk Tunnel (1375 feet) is too narrow for boats to pass but nevertheless has a towing path within it - one of the longest on the system. The shorter Whitehouses Tunnel (570 feet) has similar specifications.
Tie up north of Chirk.

Chirk Aqueduct (600 feet, 70 feet high)

Opened (1801) before its more famous neighbour, the iron trough is completely enclosed in ten masonary arches. Railway viaduct takes a parallel line but higher and wider.
Be ready for Chirk Tunnel close by.

Frankton Locks

Old branch to Llanymynech. Long term restoration aim to join up with Montgomery's isolated section.
Tie up near the junction. Walk past the restored staircase to the lock dedicated to Graham Palmer, Chairman of the Waterway Recovery Group who took

the initiative and still carries the baton.

Ellesmere Yard

British Waterways maintenance yard housed in original buildings, including the Canal Company's office - Beech House.
Tie up in the Ellesmere Branch.

Wrenbury Lift Bridge

Substantial power operated lift bridge on a busy minor road. Other lift bridges are mostly accommodation bridges for farmers.
Tie up and operate with BW key.

Hurleston Reservoir

85,000,000 gallons reserved to support the canal and subsequently for the citizens of Nantwich and Crewe. Supplied from the River Dee at Horseshoe Falls by millions of gallons a day flowing down the canal. This secondary purpose ensured the canal was maintained and never filled in during the 'dark days'.
Tie up at the top of the four lock flight.

Worth a detour

Chester

Roman port outside Roman walls. Rows, cathedral.
Tie up below the City Walls under Northgate Bridge.
16 miles, 14 locks each way. Allow 15 hours.

Nantwich

Ancient market town rebuilt in the half-timbered style after a fire in Tudor times. Fine central square
2 miles, 0 locks each way. Allow 1 hour.

Aston Locks: Montgomery Canal

Local flora and fauna became accustomed to the silted bog-like environment within the unnavigable but historic line of the canal. Volunteers have now replicated this environment in an area parallel to the canal (1993). Plants have been transferred to their new home and a final re-opening to traffic of these reconstructed locks (1985) is awaited.
Travel to Queen's Head, or further if more is open. 4 miles, 4 locks each way. Allow 4 hours plus a 2 mile walk past the Aston Locks to Maesbury. Thank the Waterway Recovery Group. Check opening times.

Pontcysyllte Aqueduct

Montgomery Canal (Isolated Section)
12 mile stretch from Guilsfield to Welshpool and Berriew passing along the edge of the Severn Valley is overlooked by Powis Castle and has trip boats, community boats and a hirebase.

Future possibilities

The final prize for tourism into Wales must be the connection of the busy Llangollen Canal with the remote sections of the Montgomery Canal via Llanymynech, Vyrnwy Aqueduct and the Prince of Wales length, to Welshpool and beyond.

i Tourist Information

Newtown Tel: 01686 625580
Welshpool Tel: 01938 552043
Llangollen Tel: 01978 860828
Ellesmere Tel: 01691 622981
Whitchurch Tel: 01948 664577

GEO Cruising Maps

GEOprojects: *Llangollen & Montgomery Canals*
GEOprojects: *Shropshire Union Canal*

Start Points

8	Alvechurch Boat Centres	**33**	Black Prince Holidays
10	Andersen Boats	**33**	Marine Services
10	Middlewich Narrowboats	**53**	Chas. Hardern & Co
13	Anglo Welsh Waterway Holidays	**54**	Cheshire Cat Narrowboat Hire
19	Anglo Welsh Waterway Holidays	**65**	Empress Holidays Ltd
20	Anglo Welsh Waterway Holidays	**85**	Maestermyn Cruisers
20	Montgomery Canal Cruises	**85**	Welsh Lady Cruisers
		121	Viking Afloat

Llangollen International Musical Eisteddfod

London Ring

Wide river and wide canal through the heart of the Capital.

Grand Union Canal - Paddington Arm (1801)
Bull's Bridge Jcn - Little Venice - Paddington Basin
Regent's Canal (1820)
Little Venice - Regent's Park - Camden Lock flight
- Islington Tunnel - Hertford Union Jcn
Hertford Union Canal (1830)
Hertford Union Jcn - Old Ford Jcn
Lee Navigation (1769)
Old Ford Jcn - Three Mills - Bow Locks
Limehouse Cut (1770, 1968)
Bow - Limehouse Basin - Limehouse Tidal Lock
Tidal River Thames
Limehouse Tidal Lock - St Katharine Docks -
Westminster - Chelsea - Putney - Mortlake - Kew -
Thames Lock, Brentford
Grand Union Canal - Main Line (1800)
Thames Locks - Hanwell Locks - Bull's Bridge Jcn

*Allow 17 hours travelling on the ring itself plus
maybe extra hours from hirebase to ring.*
*Some people will tell you that the ring can be done
in a long weekend and it can - if the tide is right.
Tides are an important element in planning because
the locks at Limehouse and Brentford only work when
the tide is right. So I suggest a week is better for a
less pressured trip and certainly if you have not
visited a big city from the waterways before.*
*Towpaths and Thames Path combine to offer a truly
fascinating and very long (45 mile) walk with such a
mix of things to see and, amazingly, hardly a road to
cross (only the short detours over the tunnels).
28 miles wide canal, 11 miles very wide tidal river
(best with two boats and a mobile phone), 3 tunnels,
23 wide locks, 2 tidal locks.*

Visiting London from the waterways is a unique
experience. Wide lock-free Paddington Arm, a
couple of tunnels, the paired locks through the
City, overnight stay in a former lighterage basin
and the passage upstream on the Thames past
familiar London landmarks on both North and
South Banks to Kew and Brentford. Finishing
with a serious flight of 7 wide locks at Hanwell.

Visitor attractions

Kensal Green Cemetery (1833)
London's first. A more commodious alternative to
overcrowded churchyards. With catacombs, grassed
walks, is full of elaborate memorials. Many of the
Victorian 'Great and Good' including Trollope,
Thackeray, Decimus Burton and I K Brunel are here.
Coffins arrived by boat, entered through a watergate.
Tie up near Bridge 5. Cross the canal.
Puppet Theatre Barge (Tel: 020 7249 6876)
One of the commercial barges around Little Venice.
Open weekends and school holidays, winter only.
London Zoo in Regent's Park (1828)
Lots of animals (650), many famous architects (ten
listed buildings including Lord Snowdon's Aviary
and Lubecian's Penguin Pool).
*Tie up near Little Venice. Catch a waterbus. Buy a
combined ticket.*
Lords Cricket Ground (Tel: 020 7289 1611)
Created from the spoil of the canal's engineering,
MCC ground offers a 'behind the scenes tour'.

*Tie up north of Maida Vale Tunnel. Walk up to Lisson
Grove and turn left.*
Madame Tussaud's Waxworks (1835)
Chamber of Horrors, Famous contemporaries.
*Tie up at Primrose Hill. Cross Regent's Park via the
Boating Lake and Inner Circle. Exit by York Gate and
turn right. A longer, but pleasant, walk.*
Camden Market
Cosmopolitan markets and redevelopments abound.
Start of regular boat trips to Little Venice and start of
the series of paired locks down to Limehouse.
Tie up just short of the locks. Very busy at weekends.
Camley Street Natural Park
Two acres of wildlife habitat - marsh, pond and
meadows. Cared for by London Wildlife Trust.
Tie up under the railway bridge.
London Canal Museum
Set in warehouse of Carlo Gatti's famous ice cream.
Before electric refridgeration was invented ship and
barge brought Norwegian ice which was stored in 40
foot deep pits to slow its melting.
Tie up in Battlebridge Basin.
Dr Barnardo's Ragged School
Museum showing East London conditions of poverty
and charitable moves to improve education in late
1800s. Lord Shaftesbury assisted.
Tie up near Lock 10.
Three Mills Visitor Centre (Tel: 020 8983 1121)
Early (1776) environmentally sound energy source.
Incoming tides are held back in a 50 acre lake and
then released under waterwheels to produce over 150
horsepower driving eight pairs of millstones.
Tie up next to the mills. Open Sunday afternoons.
Docklands Light Railway
Latest version of modern public transport, computer
controlled and now an extensive system reaching
south to Cutty Sark, Greenwich and Lewisham.
Tie up in Limehouse Basin or Poplar Dock.
Tower of London
Started by William the Conqueror, at the end of the

Trip boat at Camden Market

existing Roman Wall, it guarded the city from
seaborne attack. Watergate entry for prisoners is now
separated from the river by the new esplanade.
*Unless you have made arrangements to enter
St Katharine Docks tie up at Limehouse Basin and
catch Docklands Light Railway (Limehouse Station).*
Course of University Boat Race
Putney to Mortlake on the incoming tide. Also scene
of a greater spectacle - The Head of the River Race -
where up to 200 eight-oared boats chase one another
in a timed race over the same course.
Tie up against a pier or pontoon. This reach is tidal.

Kew Gardens
Royal Botanical Society research and 40,000 species on specimen displays. Includes the former Royal Palace and Orangery (1631), restored Palm House (1840) and 'Princess of Wales Conservatory' (1987).
Tie up above Brentford Gauging Lock. Take Thames Path back to Kew Bridge. Cross bridge to Kew Green. Main Gate is diagonally opposite.

Music Museum (Tel: 020 8560 8108)
Automatic music machines. Barrel organs, pianos, violins and a 'Wurlitzer' cinema organ.
Open summer weekend afternoons.
Tie up above Brentford Gauging Lock. Use Thames Path north along the road. Find it opposite Watermans Park.

Kew Bridge Steam Museum (Tel: 020 8568 4757)
On Green Dragon Lane. All types of pumping machinery. A 72-bucket waterwheel and five giant Cornish Pumping Engines, in steam at weekends. Small railway. Story of water supply for London.
Tie up above Brentford Gauging Lock. Take Thames Path back towards Kew Bridge.

Syon House and Park (Tel: 020 8560 0881)
Scene of two medieval battles and site of former abbey. Park has a lake, a butterfly house, a reptile house, 30 acre gardens and the Great Conservatory. 200 acre parkland landscaped by Capability Brown. House interior designed by Robert Adam.
Tie up above Brentford Gauging Lock. Use Thames Path south along the road and turn left into Park.

Osterley Park (1596, 1762) (Tel: 020 8568 7714)
Robert Adam adapted the Elizabethan mansion for the Child banking family. Contains superb examples of Georgian furniture. 140 acre landscaped park.
Tie up at the new footbridge at Boston Manor Park. Or tie up at Osterley Lock. A longer walk through woods and part of Brent River Park.

Waterway distractions

Islington Tunnel (2880 feet)
Plaques in the pavement show the way over this towpathless tunnel as canal enters City of London.
Tie up in Battlebridge Basin.

Blow-up Bridge
Disaster struck a gunpowder boat taking product from Waltham Abbey to Southall and the explosion

Westminster Bridge and Big Ben

wrecked houses around and closed down the boat company concerned (1874). The pillars were replaced wrongly - grooves previously worn by towropes rubbing outside the metal columns now appear away from the water - on the inside.
Tie up at the bridge itself.

Limehouse Tidal Lock (1820, 1869, 1989)
Barges and narrowboats crowded the basin to offload direct over the side from seagoing ships. Lock reconstructed to smaller dimensions since ships stopped calling. Nevertheless a reminder of the huge freight movements of the past.
Tie up in the basin. Give 24 hours notice of wish to use the lock to Harbourmaster (Tel: 020 7308 9930).

Thames Tidal Lock, Brentford (Tel: 020 8560 1120)
Manned Lock. Passage only possible during office hours but must coincide with the period two hours before till two hours after high tide in the Creek.
Walk round whilst waiting. Seek out Soaphouse Creek. Brentford Dock Marina was once a major transhipment depot for timber.

Worth a detour

Batchworth Lock Centre, Rickmansworth
Bull's Bridge Jcn, Cowley Peachey, Uxbridge, Denham Deep Lock, Aquedrome, Rickmansworth.

Canal exhibits, restored boats.
13 miles, 8 locks. Allow 9 hours travelling.

Thames Barrier
Turn left out of Limehouse Basin, past Canary Wharf, Docklands, Greenwich, Cutty Sark and the site of the Millennium Dome to London's huge flood protection.
6½ miles. Check the tide. Allow 5 hours travelling.

Hampton Court Palace
Upstream from Brentford, past Richmond Half Tide Lock, through Teddington Tidal Locks onto the tidefree Thames. Arrive at the palace, as the owners did in its heyday, by river.
10 miles, 2 tidal locks. Check the tide. Allow 6 hours travelling.

Short cut
Hertford Union Jcn - direct to - Limehouse Basin. To knock 1½ miles off the journey it is possible to ignore the loop via the Lee Navigation to Three Mills. A pity, as it does not reduce the number of locks and only saves half an hour - unless you include the time you might have spent investigating the Three Mills area or Old Ford Nature Reserve.
2 miles, 4 locks. Allow half an hour travelling.

Future possibilities
Soon it will be possible to tie up in a massively redeveloped Paddington Basin. This is so close to the Bakerloo, District and Circle Underground lines that it will be the perfect base for spending a couple of nights as a tourist in London.

i **Tourist Information**
London Tourist Board
Tel: 09068 663344 *(Premium rate line)*
Website: www.londontouristboard.com

Cruising Maps
GEOprojects: *Grand Union Canal map 3, Fenny Stratford to the Thames*
GEOprojects: *Thames, the river and the path*
GEOprojects: *Lee and Stort Navigations with the East London Ring*

Start Points
2	Adelaide Marine	**68**	Ferryline Cruisers
2	London & Home Counties Narrowboat Holidays	**130**	Chertsey Meads Marine

Canal Cavalcade, Little Venice, early May Bank Holiday

Lancaster Canal
Reaching towards the Lake District.

Northern Reaches (1819-1962)
 Kendal - Tewitfield (currently unnavigable)
Lancaster Canal - Long Pound (1797)
 Tewitfield - Lune - Lancaster - Glasson Jcn - Preston
Ribble Link - River Douglas Navigation
 Haslam Park - 3 rise staircase - Savick Brook -
 Tidal River Ribble - Tarleton Tidal Lock

Allow 12 hours travelling the single pound from Preston to Tewitfield. The canal will never be part of a ring, so all hirings require a return to home base (thus a current maximum of 28 hours travelling, with the possibility of many side trips by public transport). 42 miles of wide canal, 3 mile branch. 3 aqueducts, 6 wide locks to Glasson.

A peaceful isolated canal running through rustic Lancastrian countryside and passing close to the county town until the hills start to come close in anticipation of a National Park. Uniquely, no locks.

Visitor attractions

Morecombe Bay
Sandy beaches of the shallow Morecombe Bay make a wide open panorama at low tide where once a coach and four made the short journey across the sands.
Tie up near Bridge 118 at Hest Bank.

Judges' Lodgings
Once used only twice a year. Prosperous family home from 1700s displayed in a 1612 town house. Barry Elder doll collection.
Tie up on Lancaster's moorings near Bridge 99.

Avenham Park
Alongside the Ribble, the line of the original tramway river crossing can still be followed along a reproduction in concrete of the original timber trestle bridge - gives foot and cycle access.
Tie up at Ashton Basin. One mile walk.

Waterway distractions

'Waterwitch' trip boat (Tel: 01722 746914)
Five miles south of Kendal, the Lancaster Canal Trust runs free trips at Crookland Bridge.
Summer Sundays only.
From M6 J36, join A65 and go north to B6385.

Tewitfield Lock Flight
Abrupt end, noisy motorway. Eight stone chambers

end in weirs. Start of a 15 mile walk to Kendal.
Tie up alongside others near Capernwray Arm.

Lune Aqueduct (664 feet) (1797)
Five masonary arches cross the Lune in John Rennie's superb but simple grand design.
Tie up near Bridge 108. Walk down to the riverside.

Maritime Museum (Tel: 01542 64637)
Sea, port, fishing and canal displays in former Custom House, Lancaster (1764).
Tie up near Bridge 99 to Damside.

Long Pound (41 miles)
The longest length of canal on a single level in the country. It was the pride of the company which allowed horse-drawn 'Swift boats' purchased from Scotland to give a faster and smoother service than the competing stage coaches or railways. *No need to emulate the 3 hour Lancaster to Preston timetable.*

Original canal drawings (Tel: 01772 263039)
Over 50 original documents about the Lancaster Canal are held by the Records Office in Bow Lane. Includes original engraved plans (Ref: DDPD 25/34).
Tie up at Ashton Basin. Closed one week per month.

Preston Riversway (Tel: 01772 726711)
Preston Dock in another guise. Basin opens onto the Ribble two miles upstream from new Ribble Link.
Tie up at Ashton Basin. One mile walk or sail in!

Worth a detour

Glasson Branch (1825)
Six wide locks down to the huge sea basins.
3 miles, 6 locks, Allow 5 hours travelling.

Ribble Link to Tarleton (2002)
An adventure unlikely to be available to hireboats, this link will only be available at certain states of tide and with advice from British Waterways lock keepers. One way working in the tidal Savick Brook.
9 miles, 9 locks. Allow 12 hours travelling.

Future possibilities

Restoration of the waterway approach to Kendal and the Lake District is currently entering the agenda of The Waterways Trust.

i Tourist Information

Lancaster Tel: 01524 32878
Garstang Tel: 01995 602125
Preston Tel: 01772 253731

Start Points

22 Arlen Hire Boats   **123** Water Babies

Hotel Boats Snipe and Tauras in Glasson Basin

Lee and Stort Navigations
Two rivers through countryside near London.

Hertford Union Canal (1830)
Regent's Canal - Old Ford Lock - Victoria Park - Lee
Lee Navigation (1190, 1424, 1739, 1769, 1911)
Bow Back Rivers - Walthamstow - Waltham Abbey - Broxbourne - Feilde's Weir - Ware - Hertford
Stort Navigation (1796, 1911, 1924)
Feilde's Weir - Roydon - Harlow - Sawbridgeworth - Bishop's Stortford

Allow 12 hours travelling to Hertford plus 7 hours up to Bishop's Stortford. These rivers cannot be part of a ring, so all hirings require a return to home base (thus minimum 38 hours travelling).
Lee: 28 miles wide river. Stort: 14 miles, occasionally swiftly flowing, winding river.
34 wide locks, many power assisted.

Two parts, divided by the M25. Lee Valley Regional Park Authority has transformed the flood plain to the south with many playing fields and wildlife refuges. To the north is some of the most attractive countryside close to London, including ancient malting towns and a Norman Castle set in a Saxon county town.

Visitor attractions
Lea Valley Walk
Indicated from all the stations, follows river to Luton.
Signposts feature a Swan, uses the towpath.
Three Mills Visitor Centre (Tel: 020 8983 1121)
Early (1776) environmentally sound energy source. Incoming tides are held back in a 50 acre lake and then released under waterwheels to produce over 150 horsepower driving eight pairs of millstones.
Tie up next to the mills. Open Sunday afternoons.
Middlesex Filter Beds Nature Reserve
Most prominant of the fourteen reservoirs and filter beds that line the navigation. Waterfowl and wildlife.
Tie up at Pond Lane Bridge.
World War II pill box, Enfield Island
Concrete defender of the Royal Small Arms Factory (1804) home of the .303 Lee Enfield Rifle - a British Soldier's 'best friend' during WWII.
Just beyond the footbridge above Enfield Lock.
Waltham Abbey Royal Gunpowder Mills
Two levels of internal waterways carried the unstable gunpowder around the site. Waterwheels drove the machinery. An expanding museum open in summer.
Tie up at Waltham Town Lock. (Tel: 01992 767022).
Mark Hall Cycle Museum
Bikes from 1818. (Tel: 01279 454959).
Tie up at Harlow Mill.
Waytemore Castle Gardens
Central mound overlooks the river crossing it was built to defend. Sworder Fields and The Meads nearby.
Tie up at the head of the Stort Navigation.
Ware Riverside
High Street, Priory, Gazebos, old maltings and mills. Great Bed of Ware (almost 11 feet square) was an early 16th century advertising gimmick.
Tie up upstream of Town Bridge.
Hertford Castle
Splendid grounds include the Motte and Bailey but the only retained building is Edward IV's Gatehouse.
Tie up at the head of the Lee Navigation.

Gunpowdwer Mills, Waltham Abbey

Waterway distractions
New River (1608)
Early 23 mile conduit to bring fresh water to London
Tie up short of Lock 1. See New Gauge Intake.
Waltham Abbey Pound Lock (1577)
Short lived, first pound lock in the country built on a short (550') cut, was so successful it was destroyed by waggoners whose trade had been disrupted. Now merely a depression in the ground.
Stop at Waltham Town Lock. Look in Abbey grounds.

Worth a detour
London Canal Museum
Regent's Canal, Islington Tunnel, Battlebridge Basin.
5 miles, 7 locks. Allow 6 hours travelling.

📖 *Suggested Guide Book*
Richard Thomas *A Guide to the Lee and Stort Navigations* Planning and Amenities Forum, 1994

ℹ️ *Tourist Information*
Hertford Tel: 01992 584322
Bishop's Stortford Tel: 01279 655831
Lee Valley Park Tel: 01992 702200

🌍 *Cruising Maps*
GEOprojects: *Lee and Stort Navigations with the East London Ring*

Start Points
1 Adelaide Marine Ltd
2 Adelaide Marine Ltd
2 London & Home Counties Narrowboat Holidays

17

Birmingham Ring

Amazing transformation and industrial archaeology.

New Main Line (1827)
  Gas Street Basin - Old Turn Jcn - Smethwick Jcn
Old Main Line (1769)
  Smethwich Locks - Oldbury Jcn - Factory Jcn
Improved Main Line (1827)
  Factory Jcn - Coseley Tunnel - Horseley Fields Jcn
Wyrley and Essington Canal (1797)
  Horseley Fields Jcn - Holly Bank Basin - Birchills
  Jcn - Pelsall Common - Catshill Jcn
Daw End Branch Canal (1840)
  Catshill Jcn - Park Lime Pits - Longwood Jcn
Rushall Canal (1847)
  Longwood Jcn - Rushall Locks - Rushall Jcn
Tame Valley Canal (1844)
  Rushall Jcn - Spaghetti Jcn - Salford Jcn
Birmingham and Fazeley Canal (1789)
  Salford Jcn - Aston Locks - Aston Jcn - Farmer's
  Bridge Locks - Old Turn Jcn - Gas Street Basin

*Allow 24 hours travelling on the ring itself plus extra
hours from hirebase to ring.*
*42 miles of canal, 1 tunnel, 4 aqueducts, 52 narrow
locks.*

A new world - the reason the canals were built has
all but gone and we have instead an almost rural
environment interspersed with amazing industrial
archaeology and spectacular engineering.
Symphony Hall and the night life around Broad
Street. Industrial museums galore, including the
'must see' Black Country Living Museum, reward
the modern traveller.

   Maybe not for first time boaters - it is a bit of a
challenge. Hirebases are thin on the ground and so
the first challenge is up a long lock flight onto the
practically level plateau that supports Birmingham
and many of the towns which comprise the adjacent
Black Country. The Birmingham canal system
(although properly known as the Birmingham
Canal Navigations - or BCN) serves the whole of
the plateau, that is much more than Birmingham
alone, but consisting generally of two major levels
of water (453' and 473') separated by sets of three
locks at a time.

Visitor attractions

Brindley Place / Gas Street Basin
Heart of Birmingham with restaurants, bars, cafés,
museums, theatres, galleries and huge pedestrian
shopping areas.
Tie up near Broad Street Bridge.

Soho House (Tel: 0121 554 9122)
Former home of Matthew Boulton - the industrialist
financier behind James Watt's patent steam engines.
Meeting place of the Lunar Society - a hotbed of
ideas which drove the industrial revolution.
Tie up near Hockley Port, Soho Loop. Use Lodge Rd.

Galton Valley Canal Heritage Centre
Sandwell's museum about the area's industrial
heritage with varied collection of canal exhibits.
Tie up near Brasshouse Lane. Cross over north.

Black Country Living Museum
Period dress, old money, tram rides. Vast collection
of real buildings brought together into a village after
being dismantled from redevelopment sites all over
the Black Country. Seek out the lime kilns to see
huge scale of Lord Ward's industrial operation
(1778). No wonder the woods above are pockmarked
like a WWI battlefield.
Tie up actually in the museum itself.

Rough Wood Country Park
Nature Reserve on both sides of the canal. Footbridge
over leads to many footpaths through the trees.
Tie up at Bentley Wharf Bridge.

Pelsall Common
Another area reclaimed from coal mines and
ironworks. Interpretation board tells the story.
Tie up at Pelsall Works Bridge.

Discovery Centre at Millennium Point
Fun with light, sound, air, pendulums and gyroscopes. City of Birmingham, the oldest working steam engine in the world, cars, motor cycles all installed in a brand new Lottery assisted relocation of an earlier canalside glorious Museum of Science and Industry. Now needs a longer walk.
Tie up at the top of Farmer's Bridge Locks.

Waterway distractions
Gas Street Basin and Worcester Bar
Heart of Birmingham's canals. A basin where two canals did not quite join for 46 years. Now connected by a narrow disused 'stop-lock' (1815). Water buses.
Tie up on towpath near the basin itself.
Engine Arm
Original Boulton and Watt Steam Pumping Engine lifted water from the level of Telford's New Line to the summit of Brindley's Old Line for 120 years. The arm connected to Rotton Park Reservoir (1826). Superb Telford iron aqueduct cast, like many on the canal system, at Horseley Iron Works, Tipton.
Need to reverse out if you are over 30 feet long.
Galton Bridge (1829, now traffic-free)
Telford's 150 foot cast iron arch is 71 feet above the canal. The longest single span bridge of its time.
Tie up at Roebuck Lane.
Netherton Tunnel (1858)
Double width tunnel, towpath on each side - links east and west BCN canals bypassing Dudley Tunnel.
Tie up nearby. Look over the parapet.
Dudley Tunnel Trips (Tel: 0121 520 5321)
Electric boats take you into Lord Ward's cavernous limestone quarries that he linked together to create a way out west for his lime and coal. Thus for some time he avoided paying BCN's exorbitant dues.
Tie up inside the museum. Tickets at tunnel mouth.
Chillington Wharf
Railway companies created basins where goods were transferred from rail to boat. This gave them access to customers who already had their own 'sidings', ie - wharves fronting the canals. This is one of the few remaining, set in an authentic industrial landscape.
Tie up at Bilston Road Bridge.

Holly Bank Basin
Saved through the efforts of the Birmingham Canal Navigations Society
Tie up at Knight's Bridge.
Birchills Canal Museum
Housed in a former 'Boatman's Rest' provided as an antidote to visiting a pub at the day's end (1900).
Tie up near Walsall Top Lock.
Northwood Bridge
Not a wood at all. 'Utopia' blue bricks came out of the tremendous hole that now edges very close to the canal. 'Brick Kiln Pool' and 'The Swag' are similar holes but filled with water.
Tie up at Northywood Bridge. Look over the edge.
Salford Junction
Crazy memorial to centuries of engineering. A river bridged by a road (since 1290). Two canals make a junction and bridge over the river (1789). Over the top of the lot, see the many levels of bridges erected to cope with the needs of speeding road vehicles, the Spaghetti Junction slip roads for M6 / A38(M).
Tie up, look up, avoid the drips.
Farmer's Bridge Locks
The 'Old Thirteen'. Once the busiest lock flight in the country, Illuminated for 24 hour working with very early gas 'street' lighting.
Secret route, few overlooking roadways.

Worth a detour
The Crow (1837)
Six locks to the highest level on the BCN (511 feet) at Titford Pools. Check with British Waterways that there is enough water. (Tel: 0121 506 1300).
½ mile, 6 locks. Allow 4 hours travelling.
Walsall Town Wharf
Down Walsall Locks and into the refurbished basin.
½ mile, 8 locks. Allow 5 hours travelling.
Anglesey Branch and Ogley Junction
Access to Chasewater Leisure Park. Nature trails, children's boats, light railway and huge lake built to supply the canals. Water was sold to the Birmingham Canal Company.

See Ogley Junction, the turn for Lichfield in the past and in the future. Not, I am sorry to say, at

Snow Hill Arches on Farmer's Bridge Flight, BCN

present. Restoration schemes proceeding.
2¼ miles, 0 locks. Allow 1½ hours travelling.

Short cut
To cheat a little (and avoid 37 locks) it is possible to stay on the plateau by turning right at Rushall Junction and returning to the New Main Line at Pudding Green Junction via Ryders Green Locks (only 8!). Then you can return to Gas Street Basin via Smethwick Junction, perhaps avoiding all of Brindley's 'loops' on the way.
Allow 5 hours.

Future possibilities
Restorations from Huddlesford Junction to Ogley Junction on the Anglesey Branch and from Hatherton Junction up the former branch to Churchbridge, plus a new link to the Cannock Extension will create a new waterways route across the north of the plateau. Roughly one third along existing canals, it will allow two extra ways of climbing onto the plateau and thus increase the number of start points.
Previously threatened by the building of a new super-highway, a long exhausting campaign putting a case to the Government has borne fruit.
Lichfield and Hatherton Canals Restoration Trust Website: www.lhcrt.cwc.net

📖 **Suggested Guide Book**
Kevin Maslin: *Finding your way around the BCN* also website at: *www.bcn-society.org.uk*

ℹ️ *Tourist Information*
Birmingham Tel: 0121 693 6300
Dudley Tel: 01384 812830
Wolverhampton Tel: 01902 312051

🗺️ *Cruising Maps*
GEOprojects: *Birmingham Canal Navigations*

Start Points
63	Countrywide Cruisers	**119**	Viking Afloat
105	Sherborne Wharf	**124**	Water Travel Ltd

Traditional working boats at Black Country Living Museum

Monmouthshire and Brecon Canal

Many mountain panoramas, few locks.

Brecknock and Abergavenny Canal
(1812, 1865-1933, 1970)
Brecon - Talybont - Llangynidr - Llangattock - Govilon - Goytre - Pontymoile Jcn
Monmouthshire Canal (1796, 1865-1962, 1995)
Pontymoile Jcn - Sebastopol - Cwmbran

Allow 15 hours to travel the length from the basin at Brecon to the (closed) top lock at Pontnewydd in Cwmbran, adding the return journey gives a total of 30 hours. This is a week's travel at 5 hours per day but not everybody covers the whole canal. There is so much exploration possible along old tramroads and walks up into the mountains.

Shallow in places with sharp bends, it is slower than most, but it matters not.

35 miles of narrow canal, 2 tunnels, 11 aqueducts, 4 lift bridges and 6 narrow locks.

The valley of the River Usk carves its way through the mountains to Newport and this canal clings high up on Usk Valley sides for much of the way.

It twists and turns through some of the sharpest bends on the system but stays away from settlements.

It is so unconnected with any other waterway that boat owners who seek to enjoy the Brecon Beacons National Park have to use one of the hirebases. Thus six bases continue to thrive - one even offers the silence of electric propulsion.

Visitor attractions

Brecon Beacons National Park
519 square miles of breathtaking mountains reaching up to heights of over 2000 feet. Majority of the canal is within the Park and it was the park authorities who sponsored its restoration to navigable status (1970).

Many recognised walks around moors and bogs. Other discoveries to be made off the beaten track. Bike hire, potholing, pony trekking, paragliding. Otters, water voles in the valleys, wheeling peregrine falcons and breeding red kites in the skies.
Tel: 01873 853254, *Website: www.breconbeacons.org*
Tie up anywhere. The park is all around. On Sundays take 'Beacon Buses' from the Bulwark in Brecon.

Brecon (Charter 1246)
Theatre Brycheiniog, café, bar, eclectic entertainments. Priory church was 'half church of God, half castle against the Welsh'. Heritage Centre in the cathedral grounds tells the story. Jazz festival in August.
Tie up in the terminal basin (Tel: 01874 625557).

Waterfolk Canal Museum
Original Acts of Parliament and other elements from the history of these two canals are preserved in the Old Store House. Base for horse-drawn trip boat
Tie up at Bridge 158.

Talybont Reservoir
Large lake, trout fishing and twitching. Man made water to supply Newport's citizens.
Tie up at Bridge 147. Follow the Taff Trail.

Llangorse Lake
365 acres natural water, sailing, angling, twitching.
Tie up at Bridge 131. Five mile walk.

Tretower Court and Castle
Fortified manor house set around a courtyard inspired writings by Henry Vaughan (1622-1695).
Home for 350 years of the Picard family after living for 200 years in the sparse motte and bailey castle nearby. Finely dressed stonework and ornate woodwork on fireplaces and roof timbers.
Tie up near Bridge 131 or Bridge 117.
Cross the Usk by Llangynidr Bridge or Crickhowell Bridge. Roughly a 3 mile walk from either.

Crickhowell Bridge
One mile away from the canal a 12/13 arch medieval bridge crosses the River Usk. Picnic site nearby.
Tie up near Llangattock Wharf.

Llangattock Lime Kilns
Kilns and wharf allowed direct loading into boats of this early agricultural fertiliser. Huge cave systems (Agen Allwedd has 11 miles) remain in the hills.
Tie up near the wharf. Excellent walks for miles up into the hills. Pony trekking.

Crug Hywel (1480 feet)
Overlooking Rivers Usk and Grwyne Fechan. Iron age defence, modern panoramas.
Tie up at Llangattock. Strenuous 5 mile walk.

Big Pit National Mining Museum
(Tel: 01495 790311) (1860, 1880-1980, 1983)
Go 300 feet underground with experienced miners.
Wander round pit baths, water-balance lift, ovens,
five furnaces.

Early iron works (1789, 1860). 16 scheduled
ancient monuments, 82 listed buildings. Blaenavon
Industrial Landscape World Heritage Site.
Tie up at Tod's Bridge, Llanfoist. Turn under the
canal to follow the line of Hills Tramroad (1812),
stone 'sleepers' remain, three inclined planes, but
avoid the long horse tunnel (2400 feet).
Or tie up at Bridge 97, take a taxi along B4246.

Abergavenny Castle and Museum
Norman Keep in meadows with displays about the
town from prehistoric times to the present. Where
Welsh Chieftains were murdered at a Norman meal.
Tie up at Llanfoist. Cross the bridge to Abergavenny.

Goytre Hall Wood (Tel: 01873 881069)
Small woodland park and visitor centre.
Tie up at Goytre Wharf. Walk for 600 yards.

Pontypool Park and Valley Inheritance Centre
Hanbury family home park with Folly Tower rebuilt
1992 following MOD demolition during WWII.
(Tel: 01495 752036)
Tie up at Bridge 53. Footpaths fan away from the end
of the road. Access to town centre.

Waterway distractions

Brecon Basin (40 boats 1997)
Water for canal is taken from a weir on a branch of
the River Usk upstream. Beyond the weir, splashcats
and rowing boats available for hire.
Tie up in one of two basins. Walk to town, down Ship
Street, over Watergate and along the Promenade.

THE WATERFALL

Dear stream! Dear bank, where often I
Have sate and pleas'd my pensive eye,
Why, since each drop of thy quick store
Runs thitherwhence it flow'd before,
Should poor souls fear a shade or night
Who came, sure, from a sea of light?
Or since those drops are all sent back
So sure to thee, that none doth lack,
why should frail flesh doubt any more
That what God takes, he'll not restore?

Middle stanza of a poem inspired by the Usk Valley
Henry Vaughan (1622-1695)

Brynich Aqueduct (1797)
Four arches cross the deep gorge, rock cuttings.
Salmon leap in the river below. Magnificent.
Tie up near Bridge 162. Walk the towpath.

Talybont Bascule Bridge
Difficult area for the restoration. Bascule Lift Bridge
144 was needed to replace a flattened bridge (1970).
The concrete lining to the canal is the repair after a
serious breach which sent water flooding down onto
the houses below (1994).
Tie up short - power operated, BW key needed

Talybont Wharf
One of many along the canal which acted as
terminals for tramways bringing limestone, coal and
iron for transhipment. Others are at Llangattock,
Gilwern, Govilon and Llanfoist. Wharfside lime kilns
still evident, Bryn Oer Tramroad now a footpath.

Brecon Beacons from Llangynidr

Tie up near the wharf.

Ashford Tunnel (1125 feet)
Short tunnel with low roof but without towpath.
Horse path over the hill has turned into the B4558.
Short enough to see the end.
Take care of the low roof a third of the way through.

Llangynidr Locks
Run of five locks with ladders - two separate and then
three in the woods. The only set on the canal. Slightly
wider than the normal narrow locks.
Great views and low bridges.

Govilon Yard
Nerve centre of the canal, British Waterways yard in
Chief Engineer's house and yet another wharf.
Tie up near Bridge 97.

Llanfoist Wharf, Abergavenny
The tramway runs steeply up to where it collected
coal and limestone from the hills.
Tie up near Tod's Bridge. Trace the route on foot.

Sebastopol
Final mile including tunnel sponsored by the local
Council (1995) leads to a major problem of future
restoration - the 41 locks from Newport.
Tie up on the terminal moorings at Cross Keys.

📖 *Suggested Guide Book*
John Norris *The Brecon & Abergavenny section of the*
Monmouthshire & Brecon Canal John Norris, 1998

ℹ️ *Tourist Information*
Brecon Tel: 01874 622485
Crickhowell Tel: 01873 812105
Abergavenny Tel: 01873 857588
Newport Tel: 01633 842962

Start Points

28 Beacon Park Boats	**62** Country Craft
49 Cambrian Cruisers	Narrowboats
52 Castle Narrowboats	**96** Red Line Boats
	99 Road House Narrowboats

Note on Electric Boats
Electric boats turn the propeller with only a simple
whirr and the rest of the noise is from the swish of
water behind, and the gurgle of the hull passing along
the canal.

The result is that wildlife, relaxed though it is even
with normal boats, sometimes is completely unaware of
the approaching boat. If you cut the motor completely
you can drift up very close. Magic.

Electric boats were first used on the River Thames
(1889) and there are currently about 300 in Britain.

Castle Narrowboats have been using boats like
Brecon Castle, Harlech Castle, Raglan Castle and
Beaumaris Castle on this canal for over ten years.
There are recharge points at moorings along the canal.

Brecon Basin

Black Country Ring

Two river valleys and three famous lock flights.

Trent and Mersey Canal (1770)
Great Haywood Jcn - Armitage - Fradley Jcn

Coventry Canal (1790)
Fradley Jcn - Huddlesford Jcn - Fazeley Jcn

Birmingham and Fazeley Canal (1789)
Fazeley Jcn - Drayton - Salford Jcn - Aston Jcn -
Farmer's Bridge - Cambrian Wharf - Old Turn Jcn

**Birmingham Canal Navigations
(following the loops of the Old Main Line)** (1769)
Old Turn Jcn - Smethwick Jcn - Spon Lane Jcn -
Tividale - Factory Jcn - Coseley - Aldersley Jcn

Staffordshire and Worcestershire Canal (1772)
Aldersley Jcn - Autherley Jcn - Hatherton Jcn -
Gailey - Stafford - Tixall - Great Haywood Jcn

Allow 45 hours travelling on the ring.
75 miles of narrow canal, 2 tunnels, 4 aqueducts,
101 narrow locks.

Encompassing the medieval hunting forest of Cannock Chase and climbing onto the high plateau supporting Birmingham and many towns of the adjacent Black Country, the star attraction must be the Black Country Living Museum.

This route is also known as The Staffordshire Ring - as you will spend most of your time enjoying the countryside of Staffordshire.

Visitor attractions

Shugborough Hall (Tel: 01889 881388)
Lord Lichfield, photographer, is only the latest in a line of Astons who have created the Mansion House. Financed by Spanish gold, the estate has monuments and follies of Roman, Greek and Oriental inspiration.
Servants' quarters, laundry, brewhouse, butler's pantry, great kitchen, scullery, carriage houses and stables are the basis of Staffordshire County's 'Museum of Staffordshire Life'.
Tie up below Haywood Lock. Use the Packhorse Bridge to cross the River Trent.

Hopwas Hays Wood
Hanging high over the River Tame, a walk in the wood is delightful - so long as they are not using the firing range.
Tie up at Hopwas Wood Bridge. Try village moorings.

Drayton Manor Family Theme Park
Animals, gentle kids stuff and white knuckle thrills - into water and a 160 feet drop into a void - haunting.
Tie up at Coleshill Road Bridge, just opposite.

Kingsbury Water Park (Tel: 01827 872660)
20 lakes harbouring wildlife, twitchers, picnicers, walkers, paddling and adventurous children.
Tie up at Bodymoor Heath Bridge.

Brindley Place
Bright lights of Birmingham's night life. Restaurants, bars, bistros and cafés abound. Sea Life Centre and International Conference Centre with Symphony Hall. National Indoor Arena. Water buses, trip boats.
Tie up anywhere. Noise from revellers may intrude.

Black Country Living Museum
Period dress, old money, tram rides, old lime kiln. Vast collection of real buildings brought together into a village after being dismantled from redevelopment sites all over the Black Country.
Tie up actually in the museum itself.

Dudley Tunnel Trips (Tel: 0121 520 5321)
Electic boats take you into Lord Ward's cavernous limestone quarries that he linked together to create a way out west for his lime and coal. Thus for some time he avoided paying BCN's exorbitant dues.
Tie up inside the museum. Tickets at tunnel mouth.

William Perry's statue on Tipton Green
Boatmen were a competative group, arguements at locks were not unknown. William was a boatman and son of a boatman. Backed by Lord Dudley, he was English bare-knuckle boxing champion (1805-1857).
Tie up at Owen Street Bridge.

Galton Valley Canal Heritage Centre
Sandwell's museum about their extensive industrial heritage and a varied collection of canal exhibits.
Tie up near Brasshouse Lane. Cross over north.

Stafford County Town
Star of the 'Town Trail' is The Ancient High House (1595), a massive Tudor timber-framed town house, largest in England, herb garden, Shire Hall Gallery, once the Crown Court, Victorian Park, mill pond.
Tie up near Radford Bridge 98. Enter over Green Bridge (1285) site of the original ford. 2 miles.

Waterway distractions

Great Haywood Junction Bridge
Subject of a famous illustration in Eric de Maré's seminal book 'The Canals of England', published (1950) as a special number of The Architectural Review. A 'strange, remote, unearthly atmosphere'.
Tie up short of the busy junction.

Armitage Cutting (1971)
Really a former tunnel hewn in the raw rock by the picks and shovels of early navvies (1770).
Very narrow, look ahead.

Fradley Junction
Isolated canal junction and lock flight with small canal village and famous canalside pub, The Swan.
Tie up on the Coventry Canal away from the Junction.

Huddlesford Junction
Wyrley and Essington Canal was extended here (1797) and one day may be the start of a restoration serving Lichfield, Chasewater Reservoir and across to Hatherton.
Lichfield Cruising Club moorings and clubhouse.

Fazeley Junction
Alongside the A5, Watling Street. Interchange with carts and carriages. Early 5-storey Arkwright Mill.
Stop a while. See the interpretation boards.

Drayton Manor Footbridge
Oddity or folly? Both staircases of this footbridge are cased in towers.
Tie up next to the swing bridge.

Locks up to Birmingham
Eight Aston Locks plus the 'Old Thirteen' lift the canal 150 feet up to Brindley Place. Once the busiest flight in the country, the thirteen locks at Farmer's Bridge were illuminated to allow 24 hour working with very early gas 'street' lighting.

Cambrian Wharf
City centre moorings at top of Farmer's Bridge Locks.
Tie up on the 48 hour visitor moorings. Walk around.

Netherton Tunnel (1858)
Double width tunnel, towpath on each side - links east and west BCN canals bypassing Dudley Tunnel.
Tie up on Tividale Aqueduct. Look over the parapet.

Locks down from Wolverhampton
Twenty one in a single flight dropping 132 feet. Railways cross over, horses race nearby.
Tie up near Wolverhampton Top Lock.

Tixall Wide
An extravagance to appease the local gentry - the canal becomes a wide lake with wildlife galore and

Black Country Living Museum

the noisy railway is silenced by entering a tunnel to the south. Overlooked by Tixall Gatehouse.
Tie up along the towpath. Idyllic overnight moorings.

Worth a detour

Gas Street Basin
Takes hardly any time, but don't miss the old heart of Birmingham's Canals.
¼ mile, 0 locks each way. Allow half an hour.

The Bratch
Three locks in close order. Rural run.
6 miles, 9 locks each way. Allow 8 hours.

Alrewas
Canal village on the edge of growing River Trent with weirs into and out of the canal. Go for the experience - but not in winter floods.
3½ miles, 7 locks each way. Allow 6 hours.

Kingswood Junction
Pretty. Joins the wide Grand Union Canal with narrow Stratford-upon-Avon Canal. Go via Knowle and back by King's Norton.
32 miles, 31 locks for this mini ring. Allow 16 hours.

Future possibilities

Restorations from Huddlesford Junction to Ogley Junction on the Anglesey Branch and from Hatherton Junction up the former branch to Churchbridge, plus a new link to the Cannock Extension will create a new waterways route across the north of the plateau. This will allow a short cut on this Black Country Ring of about 9 hours, travelling mainly through countryside.

Previously threatened by the building of a new super-highway, a long exhausting campaign putting the case to the Government has borne fruit.
Lichfield and Hatherton Canals Restoration Trust Website: www.lhcrt.cwc.net

ℹ *Tourist Information*
Stafford Tel: 01785 619346
Lichfield Tel: 01543 252109
Tamworth Tel: 01827 311222
Birmingham Tel: 0121 693 6300
Dudley Tel: 01384 812830
Wolverhampton Tel: 01902 312051

GEO *Cruising Maps*
GEOprojects: *Trent and Mersey Canal and the River Trent map 2, Great Haywood Junction to Cromwell Lock*
GEOprojects: *Coventry and Ashby Canals and the Birmingham and Fazeley Canal*
GEOprojects: *Birmingham Canal Navigations*
GEOprojects: *Staffordshire and Worcestershire Canal with the River Severn and the Gloucester and Sharpness Canal*

Start Points

5 Alvechurch Boat Centres	**79** Jannel Cruisers Ltd
14 Anlgo Welsh Waterway Holidays	**93** Pegary Boat Hire
18 Anlgo Welsh Waterway Holidays	**105** Sherborne Wharf
36 Black Prince Holidays	**113** Swan Line Cruisers Ltd
60 Copt Heath Wharf	**114** Teddesley Boat Company
63 Countrywide Cruisers	**119** Viking Afloat
	124 Water Travel Ltd

Tixall Wide

Wey Navigation

Seriously rural waterway close to London Heathrow.

Wey Navigation (1653)
   Thames Lock - Coxes Mill - Woodham Jcn -
   Pyford - Sutton - Dapdune - Guildford Town Wharf
Godalming Navigation (1764)
   Guildford Town Wharf - Millmead - St Catherines -
   Guns Mouth - Farncombe - Godalming Wharf

Allow 8½ hours travelling the length to Godalming, adding the return journey gives a total of 17 hours, which makes the extra detours a definite possibility. 19½ miles of mixed river and cut, 16 wide locks.

Uniquely owned by the National Trust, the river is fringed by many watermeadows as it wanders about a broad Green Belt valley. It is one of the oldest river improvements in the country, accomplished over 100 years before the Duke of Bridgewater's pioneer canal arrived in Manchester. Over half the river is bypassed with artificial cuts and the locks are wide for the old Thames barges.

Visitor attractions

Coxes Mill Pond
Managed as a wildlife habitat. Mill itself (now apartments) was the last commercial user of the Wey, obtaining its grain by barge along the River Thames from London Docks (1653-1969, 1981-1983).
Tie up at Coxes Lock. Walk round the pond.

Brooklands Museum
Hugh Locke-King lived in a house on the hill and in his grounds constructed, at his own expense, the first, heavily banked, motor racing circuit that tested early cars (1907). Later 'The Magnificent Men in their Flying Machines' took off from here to get to Paris.
Tie up at Town Lock or New Haw Lock. Take a taxi.

Royal Horticultural Society: Wisley Gardens
Fantastic layout of formal, town and park gardens

Guildford Castle

with plant research and trials. Devastated by the storms of 1987, now well on the way to recovery. (Tel: 01205 549122)
Tie up short of Pyrford Bridge. Walk north then east.

Ripley Green
Old world village green in a coaching stop along the old turnpike from London to Portsmouth. Cricket, inns, restaurants and antique shops.
Tie up at Walsham, the footpath goes south.

Sutton Place
Home of Sir Richard Weston, the instigator of the river improvements and early experimenter with flooded water meadows. Once owned by Paul Getty.
Navigation flows through the private grounds.

Guildford Castle
Set in delightful grounds, at some stage the home of

the King's Government, the energetic can climb the motte (1068) and then the tower on top (1170). Great views up and down the Wey Valley.
Tie up at Millmead Lock.

Shalford Mill (National Trust)
Three storey mill powered by Tilling Brook, purchased for the nation by an anonymous group of masked women - The Furguson Gang (1932).
Tie up at St Catherine's Lock. Walk by Riff Raff Weir.

Waterway distractions

Thames Lock
Gateway to the National Trust. The Lock also has a curious additional single gate stop lock designed to raise loaded Thames barges sufficiently high to pass over the Thames Lock cill.
Tie up short of the stop lock. Consult lock keeper.

Dapdune Wharf (Tel: 01483 61389)
National Trust's exhibition and restoration of the Steven's family boatyard (1830-1963). Restored Wey barge 'Reliance' retrieved from mud-flats and refurbished (1995). Wey barge 'Perseverance IV' built here (1937).
Tie up opposite. Use the railway bridge to cross over.

Guildford Town Wharf
Town Council charged a fee for landing goods and used the money to improve the roads. Wooden crane was powered by a human treadmill.
Tie up below Town Bridge. Treadmill on the wharf.

St Catherine's Chapel
Where Chaucer's Pilgrims forded the river, or used a precarious ferry, to cross on their way to Canterbury. The Chapel was to offer prayers beforehand.
Tie up at Old Ferry Footbridge. Walk up 'Gold Hill'.

Guns Mouth: Stonebridge Wharf
18 watermills up the Tilling Brook near Chilworth were sole supplier of gunpowder to the King (1561). Barges took away the unstable cargo. Branch became the starting point of the Wey and Arun Canal leading to the South coast at Arundel.
Tie up upstream of Bradford Bridge.

Two Weeks

Holidays that last for two weeks allow everyone concerned to slow down and relax. On the waterways the extra time permits a much wider choice of routes. Many of the recognised routes are circular and known as 'rings' - six of them are described in this chapter.

Rivers and canals are both linear. Rivers flow down their valleys and canals were built between two terminii and, thus, to cruise a ring always involves more than one waterway. These contrasts are part of the attraction, river with canal, wide canal with narrow canal, following a valley or climbing a hill - most rings have a variety of types of water. It is even diffcult to avoid some industrial archaeology and some beautiful countryside within each. Most have something of everything.

Hirebases can also arrange for slightly longer holidays by combining a long weekend and a two week booking to give a total of 17 days on the boat. If you have arranged this you might also sample one of the detours suggested.

Avon Ring

Vale of Evesham and the longest lock flight.

Stratford-upon-Avon Canal (1816)
King's Norton Jcn - Brandwood - Lapworth - Kingswood Jcn - Wootton Wawen - Edstone - Wilmcote - Stratford
Upper Avon Navigation (1639, 1842, 1974)
Stratford - Bidford - Evesham
Lower Avon Navigation (1639, 1872, 1949, 1965)
Evesham - Fladbury - Pershore - Tewkesbury
River Severn Navigation (1842)
Tewkesbury - Upton upon Severn - Worcester
Worcester and Birmingham Canal (1815)
Diglis Basins - Offerton - Hanbury Jcn - Astwood - Tardebigge - Shortwood - Bittell - Wast Hill Tunnel - King's Norton Jcn

Allow 57 hours travelling.
50 miles of narrow canal, 59 miles of river, 5 tunnels, 5 aqueducts, 116 narrow locks, 18 wide locks.

Stratford-upon-Avon and Worcester are the jewels in this ring, with much to visit within a short walk of their moorings. You travel the Vale of Evesham, part of the most respected river in England and have to work the longest lock flight on the system.

Visitor attractions
Patrick Collection
Two large halls full of classic cars. Recreated 1920s street scene with early vehicles and a genuine barrel organ. The Mansell Hall has racing cars of the 1980s. Original Singer Le Mans (1934) and the James Bond prototype - the Aston Martin Zagato.
Tie up near Bridge 72, near King's Norton Junction.
Packwood House
Tudor timber-framed house. Tapestries and furniture from 1500s. (Tel: 01564 783294)
Tie up at Old Warwick Road Bridge 31. Cross and walk up to the cross roads. Use Packwood Lane.
Mary Arden's House
Childhood home to Shakespeare's mother, set out with utensils and furniture in the manner of the period. 650-hole dovecote is one of the outbuildings housing a Countryside Museum incorporating the Victorian Glebe Farm. Falcons.
Tie up near Bridge 59.
Shakespeare everywhere
His birthplace (Henley Street), his wife's place (Anne Hathaway's Cottage), his daughter's (Hall's Croft),

Site of Special Scientific Interest, Basingstoke Canal

Worth a detour

Basingstoke Canal (32 miles) (1794 - 1930, 1991)
Because alkaline water from chalk springs and acid water from the heathland creates a unique set of habitats for flora and fauna, almost the whole canal is designated a Site of Special Scientific Interest (1995) - the exception is the urban pound through Woking. Walking along the towpath is thus richly rewarding.

Backpumping recently installed on the 6 lock Woodham Flight should allow regular navigation up to Woking's modernised town shops, multiplex cinemas, Rhoda McGaw and New Victoria theatres.

Early restoration parties of volunteers played a major part in restoring this canal over 17 years, but further travel up the Deepcut Locks into the two long top pounds is more difficult. If there is ever a shortage of rain, lack of water can shut the canal. Also, in order to maintain a balance with flora and fauna that have made the canal environs their home, the Basingstoke Canal Authority has set up electronic boat counters to monitor boat movements and may refuse entry.
Check at Mytchett Canal Centre (Tel: 01252 370073).
3 miles, 6 locks to Woking and back. Allow 5 hours.
Windsor
Out onto the River Thames and turn left. Chertsey, Staines and Runnymede to Windsor. Lots to see.
11 miles, 6 manned locks each way. Allow 10 hours.
Hampton Court Palace and Maze
Out onto the River Thames and turn right. Desborough Cut, Walton, Sunbury, Molesey, Hampton Court.
6 miles, 2 manned locks each way . Allow 4 hours.

i **Tourist Information**
Guildford Tel: 01483 444333
Basingstoke Tel: 01256 817618
Fleet Tel: 01252 811151

GEO **Cruising Maps**
GEOprojects: *Basingstoke Canal*
GEOprojects: *Thames, the river and the path*

Start Points
67 Farncombe Boat House	**73** Guildford Boat House Ltd
68 Ferryline Cruisers	**83** Kris Cruisers
72 Galleon Marine	**130** Chertsey Meads Marine

Royal Shakespeare Theatre, Stratford-upon-Avon

his granddaughter's (Nash's house), his baptismal church (Holy Trinity), his school (Guildhall & Old Grammar School) and a 'World of Shakespeare' recreating the milieu of his lifetime. Also enjoy his plays.
(Royal Shakespeare Theatre, Tel: 01489 403405).
Tie up beside the river gardens at Stratford.

Pershore Abbey (689, 983, 1239, 1288)
Glorious ruins in a splendid Georgian market town.
Tie up at recreation ground. Walk into town.

Bredon Hill (961 feet)
Geologically an outlier of the Cotswold escarpment, outpost of Costwold Area of Outstanding Natural Beauty, dominates views from the river.
Tie up at Eckington Wharf. Longer vigorous walk.

Tewkesbury Abbey
Built of stone shipped from Normandy, last monastery on Henry VIII's hit list. Saved by the townspeople.
Tie up at moorings suggested by LANT lock keeper.

Upton upon Severn
Copper covered cupola reigns over early timber framed and Georgian buildings. Attractive waterside.
Moor upstream of bridge. Walkers can approach Malvern Hills from here (6 miles away).

Worcester
Elgar, Commandery, Royal Worcester Porcelain,

Worcester Cathedral presides over the oldest music festival in Europe, Three Choirs Festival, and over a city proud of its ancestors, Charles II's War Rooms, and the finest porcelain with a dash of Lee & Perrins.
Tie up above Lock 3, in the Commandery Yard.

Hanbury Hall
Ice house gave early refrigeration for a 1701 gentleman's house. William and Mary style, painted

ceilings. Porcelain collection.
Tie up near Bridge 38. Walk beyond Summer Hill.

Avoncroft Museum of Historic Buildings
Three-seater earth closet from Leominster is the smallest of the rescued and rebuilt structures. Others include local nail works, working windmill, timber-framed houses and the Guesten Hall roof from Worcester Cathedral Priory which sits on a new hall.
UK Telephone Koisk Collection (Tel: 01527 831363).
Tie up at Stoke Wharf, or Bridge 48 . Walk north.

Waterway distractions

King's Norton Stop Lock
A guillotine lock erected to stop one canal company's water flowing continuously into the other's channel. Connection was only made when a boat passed through taking just a small amount of water with it.
Now both are BW, so the guillotine is always up.

Lapworth Locks and Kingswood Junction
First flight out from Birmingham drops past a wide storage lake and a link to the broad Grand Union Canal.
Tie up for a moment and wander around the towpaths.

Edstone Iron Aqueduct (754 feet)
Longest of three cast-iron aqueducts. Towpath set so low as to give a fishes' eye view of passing boats.

Tie up and walk the towpath.

Bancroft Basin (1858)
The Bancroft is large parkland built over a disused terminal basin similar in size. Headroom of Bridge 69 into the operative basin is low because the one-way road system had to be rebuilt to allow restoration.
Tie up in the basin, walk back to the pub.

Stratford and Morton Horse Tramway Bridge
Goods were transhipped from two Bancroft Basins onto an early 'railway' (1826) which went almost 20 miles to Morton-in-Marsh. One of its wagons stands beside the basin.
Walk across the narrow bridge (1823) and follow the Old Tramway. Walk southwards.

Anonymous Lock
Acknowledgement of the way that many donations

toward the Upper Avon restoration were made. A single gift amounted to almost one third of the estimated costs at the time.
Tie up, look at the memorial.

Pershore Bridges (Great 1300s, New 1928)
Two bridges built 600 years apart but so close as to create turbulance when assaulted by spring waters.
Take largest arch of Great Bridge and central on New. Arrive by car to the picnic site on A44.

Diglis Basins
Wide locks lead up into the basins, allowing haven to River Severn boats. Two basins are full of moored craft of many differing types. Regeneration scheme.
Tie up on towpath below Bridge 2.

Hanbury Junction
Droitwich Junction Canal leads to Droitwich Spa and the Droitwich (Barge) Canal (see page 8).
Walk down to see Waterway Recovery Group works.

Tardebigge Locks
Thirty locks climbing 217 feet plus the six at Stoke - provides a baptism of fire - 36 locks in four miles. They are close enough for a crew member to walk forward to prepare the next lock whilst the current lock is filling. Or, if you have a bicycle, you can go quicker and further - technical term - 'lock wheeling'.
But look to see if boats coming the other way will pass through and thus set the next lock for you anyway.

Aickman - Rolt Plaque
The BW maintenance depot prevents the top lock of the Tardebigge flight being in the middle of nowhere, a bleakness especially noted by Robert Aickman in 1946. He had walked from Bromsgrove station to meet his fellow author Tom Rolt living here with his wife Angela on their narrowboat 'Cressy'. The meeting led to the founding of the Inland Waterways Association which campaigned for over 50 years for the Government to recognise all inland waterways as an asset not a liability. Present Government now accepts this view and encourages everyone to use the water, hedgerows and towing paths for the recreational opportunities they offer.
IWA commemorative plaque tells the story by Lock 58.

River Avon at Tewkesbury

Worcester and Birmingham Canal Tunnels
Tardebigge (1740 feet), Shortwood (1840 feet) and Wast Hill (8179 feet) are grand wide structures on the summit pound built when it was thought the complete route would be for wide barges.

Worth a detour

Stourport Basins
Continue upstream on the Severn to a Georgian town.
13 miles, 3 locks each way. Allow 8 hours.

Gas Street Basin and Worcester Bar
Worcester and Birmingham Canal's 20 year stand-off with the Birmingham Canal Campany meant double handling across the 7 foot Worcester Bar. Go and pass through the disused stop lock. Today's attractions are pubs and clubs clustered around the heart of the canal system.
Up by the Worcester and Birmingham Canal from King's Norton Junction and back along the Warwick and Birmingham Canal to Kingswood Junction. 20 miles, 26 narrow locks and 5 wide locks, 1 tunnel. 13 hours but saves 7 hours so extra 6 hours.

Hatton Locks
A quick look at a flight of wide locks (rebuilt 1935).
5 miles, 1 tunnel each way. Allow 2½ hours.

ℹ️ Tourist Information
Stratford-upon-Avon Tel: 01789 293127
Evesham Tel: 01386 446944
Tewkesbury Tel: 01684 295027
Upton upon Severn Tel: 01684 594200
Worcester Tel: 01905 726311
Droitwich Spa Tel: 01905 774312

🗺️ Cruising Maps
GEOprojects: *Staffordshire and Worcestershire Canal with the River Severn and the Gloucester and Sharpness Canal*
GEOprojects: *Worcester and Birmingham Canal with the Droitwich Canals*
GEOprojects: *Birmingham Canal Navigations*
GEOprojects: *Grand Union Canal map 1, Birmingham to Fenny Stratford*
GEOprojects: *Stratford-upon-Avon Canal and the River Avon (2002)*

Start Points
5	Alvechurch Boat Centres	66	Evesham Marina Holidays
18	Anglo Welsh Waterway Holidays	80	Kate Boats Warwick
21	Anglo Welsh Waterway Holidays	93	Pegary Boat Hire
31	Bidford Boats	105	Sherborne Wharf
36	Black Prince Holidays	109	Starline Narrowboats
44	Brook Line Narrowboat Holidays	110	Stroudwater Cruisers
60	Copt Heath Wharf	115	Telstar Cruisers Ltd
		122	Viking Afloat

Lapworth Locks, Stratford-upon-Avon Canal

Cheshire Ring
Peak National Park and river valleys.

Bridgewater Canal (1765, 1773)
    Preston Brook Jcn - Bollin Embankment - Waters
    Meeting - Castlefield Jcn
Rochdale Canal (1804)
    Castlefield Jcn - Rochdale Nine - Ducie Street Jcn
Ashton Canal (1796)
    Ducie Street Jcn - Portland Basin - Dukinfield Jcn
Peak Forest Canal (1800)
    Dukinfield Jcn - Woodley and Hyde Bank Tunnels
    - Marple Aqueduct - Marple Locks - Marple Jcn
Macclesfield Canal (1831)
    Marple Jcn - Bollington Aqueduct - Bosley
    Locks - Red Bull Aqueduct - Hardings Wood Jcn
Trent and Mersey Canal (1777)
    Hardings Wood Jcn - Middlewich Locks - Anderton
    Lift - Preston Brook Tunnel - Preston Brook Jcn

Allow 55 hours travelling.
30 miles wide canal, 72 miles narrow canal, 102 total
miles including a 40 mile lock free pound.
4 tunnels, 2 aqueducts, 83 narrow locks, 9 wide locks.
Seven Wonders: Anderton Lift.

**Created after early successful campaigns for the
repair of a canal breach and the restoration of key
segments (1968, 1971, 1972) this is one of the
original cruising rings.**

It takes you though gentle Cheshire Countryside
and passes by rearing gritstone escarpments but at
its heart is metropolitan Manchester with lots of
places to visit within half an hour of moorings.

It climbs past the Pennines to some of the
highest water in the country and drops down close
to the tidal Mersey. It includes two early canals
and one from the end of the first canal mania age.

Some try to race round the circuit in a week
travelling for most daylight hours, but I believe
that leaves too few hours for coming onto land.

Visitor attractions

Dunham Massey Hall
250 acre deer park, beech avenues, working
Elizabethan mill - 30 room mansion with furniture,
paintings, silver, kitchen, laundry and stables.
Tie up near Bridge 27.
Old Trafford (Tel: 0161 872 0199)
Manchester United Museum and Trophy Room.

Little Morton Hall

Tie up at Throstle Nest Footbridge (Bridge 96).
Museum of Science and Industry (Tel: 0161 872 0199)
Celebrating the saying 'what Manchester does today,
the world does tomorrow'. Includes exhibits of early
computers, aviation, printing and textile machinery.
Tie up near Castlefield Arena. Allow a few hours.
Granada Studios Tour
Coronation Street and all that jazz.
Tie up near Castlefield Arena. Allow a few hours.
Metrolink Trams
Comfortable public transport as it should be.
Tie up near Castlefield Arena. Use G-Mex Tram stop.
Bridgewater Hall (Tel: 0161 907 9000)
Home of Halle Orchestra. Foyers open 7 days a week.
Tie up near Lock 89 or enter the basin.
Velodrome
Cradle of some of Britain's Olympic cyclists.
Tie up near Lock 8 on the Ashton Canal.
Lyme Park
1377 acre deer park, Lyme cage folly, costumed
attendants, gardens, fishing, horseriding.
Tie up near Bridge 15. A longer walk east.
Paradise Mill, Macclesfield
Fine work in silk from the country's leading centre.
Tie up at Bridge 40.
Mow Cop Trail
Energetic waymarked walk to 'The Cloud' and super
views across the Cheshire Plain.
Tie up at Bridge 72.
Little Morton Hall (National Trust)
Fine timber-framed manor house (1500s) with long
wainscoted gallery, chapel, priest's hole, furniture
knot garden and moat.

Tie up at Bridge 85. Get there before the coaches.
Salt Museum, Northwich (Tel: 01606 41331)
Creator of flashes, destroyer of buildings, underminer
of canals (1958), supplier of essential life force. Tales
of salt working since Roman times.
Tie up at Bridge 184. A longer walk west.

Waterway distractions

Lymm Dam
Fishermen surround this water set in idyllic
surroundings. Supply reservoir for the canal.
Tie up at narrow A6144 Lymm Bridge. Wooded walk.
Bollin Embankment
Narrowest part of the Bridgewater. A spectacular
breach (1971) forced a two year closure but a new
concrete channel was built with public money.
Tie up near Dunham.
Castlefield Basin
Series of specialised wharves for all manner of goods
brought here by the very first cross-valley canal.
Tie up alongside the events arena.
Salford Quays and River Irwell
Manchester Ship Canal is no longer big enough for
today's ships but lock down, turn right, go past the
former entrance to the Manchester, Bolton and Bury
Canal up to the limit of river navigation by the Mark
Addy pubside moorings. Turn left and tie up near The
Lowry in one of the vast docks built at the end of the
canal for 20th century ships. (Tel: 0161 872 2411)
*Drop down to the river through Pomona Lock. There
and back in 2 hours.*
Rochdale Nine
Wide locks pass the heart of Manchester night life.
Chinatown and gay pubs nearby.
Two mile link that is now a passage free of charge.
Portland Basin: Tameside Heritage Museum
Industial heritage displayed in rebuilt warehouse.
Tie up in the basin. Canals Festival mid July.
Marple Aqueduct and Locks
Goyt Valley spanned by Benjamin Outram's three-
arched, 100 foot high Scheduled Ancient Monument.
16 locks climb 214 feet through woods past local
parkland and leafy suburban houses.
*Tie up north of the Aqueduct. Energetic walk on
waymarked path into the valley, well worth the trouble.*
Bosley Locks
12 locks descend 118 feet in magnificent surroundings.
Telford's only locks on the Macclesfield Canal.
Heartbreak Hill
26 sets of locks were made into pairs (1835) to
reduced waiting time on this busy waterway.
Chamber of Lock 53 was rebuilt in steel after being
wrecked by salt-induced subsidence, but was heavy
to work and ignored by boatmen.
Twenty nine locks in ten miles.
Middlewich Big Lock
Sole wide lock at the north end of Trent and Mersey
Canal built to let barges away to Manchester and
Wigan but negated by the narrow tunnel at Preston
Brook and the rebuilt dimensions of Croxton Aqueduct.
*Only one stop lock until Manchester 40 miles away
or Wigan 54 miles away.*
Three Tunnels
Wide passing pounds separate Barton (1716 feet) and
Salterford (1272 feet) Tunnels. Together with Preston
Brook Tunnel (3717 feet) they allow the canal to hug
the steep side of the Weaver Valley.
*Tie up and await your hourly slot. On the hour
northbound, on the half-hour southbound.*

The Cloud from Bosley Locks

Worth a detour

Worsley Delph and Barton Aqueduct
Duke's mines at Worsley, original source of coal to Manchester. Huge Barton Swing Aqueduct built by Manchester Ship Canal Company after it bought both the Bridgewater Canal and River Irwell Navigation. *5 miles, 0 locks each way. Allow 2½ hours.*
Anderton Lift (2002) **and Weaver Navigation**
Wide navigation under huge swing bridges that let sea going cargo ships up as far as Winsford. Narrowboats pass under without disturbance. Vale

ℹ️ *Tourist Information*
Altrincham Tel: 0161 912 5931
Manchester Tel: 0161 234 3157
Ashton-under-Lyne Tel: 0161 343 4343
Macclesfield Tel: 01625 504114

GEO *Cruising Maps*
GEOprojects: *Trent & Mersey Canal map 1, Preston Brook to Fradley Junction*
GEOprojects: *Macclesfield and Peak Forest Canals with the Ashton Canal*

Start Points

7	Alvechurch Boat Centres	55	Claymoore Navigation Ltd
10	Andersen Boats		
10	Middlewich Narrowboats	59	Constellation Cruises Ltd
16	Anglo Welsh Waterway Holidays	65	Empress Holidays Ltd
32	Black Prince Holidays	77	Heritage Narrowboats
35	Black Prince Holidays	92	Peak Forest Cruisers
54	Cheshire Cat Narrowboat Hire		

Royal cut, turn at Winsford Bottom Flash.
7 miles, 2 locks each way. 5 hours plus time for passing through lift. Book the lift in advance.

Peak National Park and Bugsworth Basin
River Goyt Valley, Millennium Walkway to the Torrs, Bugsworth Basin - a huge canal/tramway interchange and major limestone source. Now under re-restoration.
7 miles, 0 locks each way. Allow 4 hours.

Harecastle Tunnel to Etruria
Experience the second longest tunnel. Go to original Wedgwood pottery site and Bone and Flint Mill.
5½ miles, 0 locks each way. Allow for waiting at the tunnel and 3 hours.

📖 *Suggested Guide Book*
Exploring the Cheshire Ring British Waterways, 2000

Leicester Ring

Glorious countryside east of Birmingham.

River Trent Navigation (1783)
  Derwent Mouth - Sawley - Trent Lock - Redhill
River Soar - Loughborough Navigation (1778)
  Redhill - Kegworth - Zouch - Loughborough
River Soar - Leicester Navigation (1794)
  Chain Bridge, Loughborough - Barrow -
  Mountsorrel - Old Jcn - Belgrave - Abbey
  Park - West Bridge
Leicestershire and Northamptonshire Union Canal
(1797, 1809)
  West Bridge - Mile Straight - Newton - Kibworth -
  Saddington Tunnel - Debdale - Foxton Jcn
'Old' Grand Union Canal (1814)
  Foxton Jcn - Husbands Bosworth - Crick - Norton Jcn
Grand Junction Canal (1796)
  Norton Jcn - Braunston Tunnel - Braunston Turn
North Oxford Canal (1774, 1834)
  Braunston Turn - Hillmorton - Hawkesbury Jcn
Coventry Canal (1790)
  Hawkesbury Jcn - Marston Jcn - Atherstone -
  Fazeley Jcn - Huddlesford Jcn - Fradley Jcn
Trent and Mersey Canal (1770)
  Fradley Jcn - Alrewas - Bond End - Willington -
  Swarkstone - Shardlow - Derwent Mouth

Allow 65 hours travelling.
29 miles of river, 40 miles of wide canal, 83 miles of
narrow canal. Total 152 miles, 99 locks.
5 tunnels, 6 aqueducts, 55 wide locks, 44 narrow locks.
Seven Wonders: Foxton Inclined Plane. See page 80.

Rivers change levels so quickly in winter, not
recommended out of season.

Visitor attractions
John Taylor Bell Foundry (Tel: 01509 223414)
World's largest bell foundry with museum which
shows moulding, casting, tuning and fitting. Works
tours occasionally.
Stop at Bridge 38. Cross, follow A60 to Freehold St.
Great Central Steam Railway (Tel: 01509 230726)

Sculpture, Market Harborough Basin

Main line steam trains to Belgrave, Birstall and back.
Tie up near Bridge 35. Cross into Great Central Rd.
Wigston Framework Knitters Museum
Aficionados hands-on. Use a frame, use a Griswold.
Tie up near Double Rail Lock. Cross and walk north.
Shardlow
Transhipment port between narrowboats and river
barges. Warehouses are in neat vernacular. (1780s)
Tie up within the village. Walk around.

Waterway distractions
Abbey Pumping Station Museum (1891)
Water - clean and foul. Shiny massive beam engine
used to pump sewage. (Tel: 0116 266 1330)
Tie up near Belgrave Lock. Cross Holden St Bridge.

Leicester Mile Straight (1890s)
Two weirs to the north, a huge one to the south and
this vast flood-prevention watercourse between, were
built by City Corporation in a very wide straight line.
Tie up at West Bridge near Castle Park. Avoid weirs.
Foxton Locks, Inclined Plane and Museum
Two staircases of five locks each. An original
inclined plane which could have done with an electric
motor. The museum explains all.
Tie up at top or bottom. Take your time to see it all.
Watford Locks
Seven narrow locks, four locks in a staircase with
side pounds and single locks above and below.
Take advice on working the paddles from lock keeper.
'Red before white and you'll be all right, White
before red, a clip round the head'.
Braunston Tunnel, Locks, village and Turn
Original wide Grand Junction Canal met end-to-end
with the narrow Oxford Canal, thus Braunston was a
transhipment spot. Pickford's wharf and depot.
Village became central to boatmen's lives.
Hillmorton Paired Locks (1840)
Only locks on the North Oxford Canal, duplicated to
speed up passage when the line was straightened.
Use either lock depending on which is set for you.
Sutton Stop at Hawkesbury
Mr Sutton checked the boats coming through.
Tie up on visitor moorings. See the improved garden.
Fradley (1774)
Tiny terrace of canal cottages overlook old junction.
Tie up on the Coventry Canal.

Worth a detour
Market Harborough
Planned 'new town' (1180s) half-timbered buildings,
old coaching inns. Site of IWA rallies 1950, 1990.
4¼ miles, 0 locks each way. Allow 2½ hours.
Bishop Street Basin, Coventry
Much improved approach to Lady Godiva's City.
5½ miles, 0 locks each way. Allow 3 hours.
Bosworth Field and Moira Furnace
Lock-free through rolling country to a famous battle
and beyond to Snarestone. Until the restoration gets
there, take a taxi to Moira Furnace and Heart of the
National Forest Centre nearby (Tel: 01283 224667).
22 miles, 0 locks each way. Allow 11 hours plus taxi.
Birmingham Bright Lights: Brindley Place
Restaurants, bars, bistros and cafés abound.
21 miles, 38 locks each way. Allow 30 hours.

ℹ️ *Tourist Information*
Loughborough Tel: 01509 218113
Leicester Tel: 0116 265 0555
Rugby Tel: 01788 571813
Nuneaton Tel: 01203 347006
Tamworth Tel: 01827 59134
Burton upon Trent Tel: 01827 59134

📖 *Cruising Maps*
GEOprojects: *Trent and Mersey Canal and the River*
Trent map 2, Great Haywood Junction to Cromwell
Lock
GEOprojects: *Grand Union Canal map 1,*
Birmingham to Kings Langley
GEOprojects: *Grand Union Canal map 4, Leicester*
Line, Soar Navigation and Erewash Canal
GEOprojects: *Oxford Canal*
GEOprojects: *Coventry and Ashby Canals and the*
Birmingham and Fazeley Canal

Coventry Cathedral

Start Points

23 Ashby Boat Company	**79** Jannel Cruisers Ltd
38 Blisworth Tunnel Boats Ltd	**80** Kate Boats Warwick
47 Calcutt Boats Ltd	**88** Napton Narrowboats
50 Canalboat Holidays Ltd	**100** Rose Narrowboats Ltd
56 Clifton Cruisers	**107** Sileby Mill Boatyard
57 Club Line Cruisers	**113** Swan Line Cruisers Ltd
57 London & Home Counties Narrowboat Holidays	**117** Union Canal Carriers Ltd
	118 Valley Cruises Ltd
	120 Viking Afloat
61 Coronet Canal Carrying Co	**120** Willow Wren Cruising Holidays
71 Foxton Boat Services Ltd	**125** Weltonfield Narrowboats Ltd
78 Ian Goode Narrowboats	

31

South Pennine Ring
Cross the magnificent Pennines twice.

Calder and Hebble Navigation (1770)
Sowerby Bridge - Salterhebble - Brighouse - Cooper Bridge Jcn
Huddersfield Broad Canal (1774)
Cooper Bridge Jcn - Locomotive Bridge - Aspley Basin
Huddersfield Narrow Canal (1779, 1811)
Aspley Basin - Staithwaite - Marsden - Standedge Tunnel - Uppermill - Stalybridge - Portland Basin
Ashton Canal (1796)
Portland Basin - Dukinfield Jcn - Ducie Street Jcn
Rochdale Canal (1804)
Ducie Street Jcn - Failsworth - Slattocks - Castleton - Rochdale - Hollingworth - Summit - Todmorden - Hebden Bridge - Sowerby Bridge

Allow 70 hours travelling on the ring.
31 miles of wide canal, 27 miles of narrow canal,
9 miles of river, 3 tunnels, 6 aqueducts, 107 wide
locks, 92 narrow locks.
Seven Wonders: Standedge Tunnel. See page 80.

Two 'frankly impossible restorations' have been brought to fruition by the tenacity and foresight of enthusiasts, aided and abetted by two wide ranging partnerships of local government and waterway organisations. This ring (Rochdale Canal open in 2002), will create a challenge to attain the heights of the Pennine Chain for crews who enjoy working locks. It will take an energetic two weeks, requiring 6 hours per day travelling.

Visitor attractions

Halifax (Tel: 01422 368725)
Eureka! - kids museum up to age of 12, Piece Hall with 315 merchants rooms, Shibden Hall (1420) and 90 acre park with bluebell woods, family attractions.
Tie up near The Quays public house.
Mikron Theatre
Famous group of narrowboat travelling players have their headquarters across the river in The Mechanics Institute, Marsden. (Tel: 01484 843701)
Tie up at Station Bridge. Walk south into town.
Standedge Experience
Exhibition entry (fee) includes an electric trip boat ride into the end of a tunnel.

Tie up before the tunnel.
Marsden Moor Estate (5600 acres, National Trust)
Evidence of stone and bronze ages, high in the hills, away from administrators, scenes of highway robbery, Wesleyan evangelism and Luddite activities. Old line of Roman road, packhorse trail, turnpike and boat lane.
Tie up near Station Bridge. (Tel: 01484 847016)
Portland Basin Museum
Industrial museum and café overlooking basin.
Tie up in the basin itself.
East Lancashire Railway (Tel: 0161 764 7790)
Steam operated line from Heywood, Bury and Rawtenstall. Go by train from Castleton station.
Tie up above Bluepit Lock Flight.
Healey Dell, Rochdale
Nature Trail in deep clough. Waterworn rocks, woods, waterfalls, rushes, ferns, mosses, orchids.
Tie up at Clegg Hall Bridge. Longer walk west.
Hollingworth Lake (Tel: 01706 373421)
Two miles around, three dams and a Victorian Tourist Resort. Visitor Centre with interpretation boards.
Stop at Heald Lane Bridge. Cross, walk eastwards.
Roman Road, Littleborough
So well preserved it might be remains of a turnpike, but is on a straight line from Manchester and Ilkley. Such 'roads' were for marching soldiers - heavy goods were probably taken to Roman Forts by barge.
Tie up downstream of Sladen Lock 44. Cross bridge and climb to A58.
Pennine Way
Long distance footpath, 210 miles north to Kirk Yetholm, Northumberland and, going south, 10 miles to Standedge Tunnel, 40 miles to Edale, Peak District.
Crosses the Rochdale Canal at Callis Lock.
Heptonstall
Typical hill top village with cottages for 'outworker' weavers. Waymarked nature trail.
Tie up above Lock 11. Cross A646 and climb hill
Hebden Bridge
'Pennine Centre' with a stone bridge (1510) over the river and a warm welcome to the restored canal. Craft shops, new marina with Pace-Egging by mummers every Good Friday.
Tourist Information close to canal. Tie up near Lock 9.
Walkley's Clogs
Exhibitions of clog manufacture, coin counterfeiting and an 'Enchanted Wood'. (Tel: 01422 842061)
Tie up north of Fallingroyd Tunnel.

Waterway distractions
Tuel Lane Lock (19'6")
Deepest in the country, replacing two original locks. Approached by a new tunnel, it has separate sets of bottom gates for both the Calder boats and the 72 foot standard 'Midland' boats. (Tel: 01422 316678)
Ring lock keeper before proceeding into tunnel.
Calder and Hebble Navigation
Originally only riverside horsepaths and short cuts around problem reaches, it was slowly improved to become a canal playing bib and tuck with the river.
Be aware of water currents from weir overflows.
Halifax Branch (1828)
14 locks in 1½ miles is too much to restore and only ever worked via an expensive back-pumping operation with over 100 feet lift. Waymarked 'Hebble Trail' follows the many mills along Hebble Brook past 10 derelict lock sites to Piece Hall.
Turn into branch, tie up at The Quays public house.
Huddersfield Broad Canal
Alternative name for Sir John Ramsden's private canal built to open up his lands to Yorkshire Keels.
Tie up at the terminus - Aspley Basin.

Hebden Bridge

Standedge Tunnel (Tel: 01484 844298)
Longest tunnel in the country (17,000 feet), hewn through living rock 638 feet below gound and 645 above the sea. 3½ hours to go through.
Tie up before the tunnel. Pre-book your passage £35.
Seats on crew boat for non-boaters also available £6.
Manchester's Orbital Motorway, Chadderton.
Not strictly a waterway distraction, but this diversion and box culvert reflects an early (1986) success at a public inquiry into the building of a new major road. Well before recent (2001) Government instructions to road builders to include crossings of future canal restorations in their designs.
Note the narrow specification and a separate towpath route over M60.
Ellenroad Engine House (Tel: 01706 881952)
Protects a survivor from hundreds of steam engines that were central power sources for mill looms and other machinery. Twin tandem compound engine produces 3000 horsepower. 220 foot chimney.
Tie up at Minnow Road Bridge. Long walk to M62 J21. Open Sundays.

Cross section through Huddersfield Broad and Narrow Canals
(height in feet above mean sea level)

(Cross section diagram labels:)
(Peak Forest Canal) · Dukinfield Junction · ASHTON-UNDER-LYNE · STALYBRIDGE · Scout Tunnel · Locks 1-32W · MOSSLEY · DIGGLE · 1283 feet (summit) · Standedge Tunnel (638 feet below ground) · MARSDEN · Locks 1-42E · HUDDERSFIELD Aspley Basin · (Calder & Hebble Navigation) Cooper Bridge Junction

Huddersfield Narrow Canal — < 3½ miles > — *Huddersfield Broad Canal*

distance in miles

Saddleworth, Huddersfield Narrow Canal

Blackstone Edge Canal Reservoirs (1827)
Over 600 feet above the canal summit, seven separate reservoirs collect rain from 2000 acres of moors to feed Rochdale and Oldham and the canal below.
Tie up near Warland Gate Bridge. Long climb east to join the Pennine Way along Blackstone Edge past Warland, Light Hazzles and White Holme Reservoirs.

Longlees Lock 36
One end of the summit pound at 600 feet above sea level, restored (1979) by the Rochdale Canal Society in the days when such efforts were a supreme act of faith. Give thanks and £6 for a Summit Brass Plaque.
Summit pound is wide and deep, passing through the greatest scenery. Turnpike nearby, rail tunnel below.

Great Wall, Todmorden (1858)
Railway sidings squeezed into the valley supported by this sheer wall of tens of thousands of bricks.
Tie up at Lock 19.

Fallingroyd Tunnel
No towpath, but the trip boat is horse-drawn - so look out for the slow 'legging' process inside the tunnel.
When entering the tunnel, be aware, take care.

Worth a detour
Castlefield Basin
Do not miss this series of specialised wharves for all manner of goods built here by Duke of Bridgewater.
2 miles, 9 locks each way. Allow 6 hours.

Barton Aqueduct and Worsley Delph
Duke's mines at Worsley, original source of coal to Manchester. Huge Barton Swing Aqueduct built by Manchester Ship Canal Company after it bought Bridgewater Canal Company to control River Irwell.
7 miles, 9 locks each way. Allow 9 hours.

Marple Aqueduct and Bugsworth Basin
River Goyt Valley, Millennium Walkway to the Torrs, Bugsworth Basin - a huge canal/tramway interchange and major limestone source. Now under re-restoration.
14 mile, 16 locks each way. Allow 15 hours.

📖 *Suggested Guide Book*
John Lower *The South Pennine Ring* Hallamshire, 1998

ℹ️ *Tourist Information*
Halifax Tel: 01422 368725
Huddersfield Tel: 01484 223200
Manchester Tel: 0161 234 3157
Rochdale Tel: 01706 356592
Hebden Bridge Tel: 01422 843831

🗺️ *Cruising Maps*
GEOprojects: *Huddersfield Broad and Narrow Canals with the Ashton Canal*
GEOprojects: *South Pennine Ring* (2002)

Start Points
16 Anglo Welsh Waterway Holidays
24 Aspley Wharf Marina
55 Claymoore Navigation Ltd
59 Constellation Cruises Ltd
104 Shepley Bridge Marina Ltd
106 Shire Cruisers

Stourport Ring
Kinver Edge and Birmingham bright lights.

Birmingham Canal Navigations (1769-1863)
  Aldersley Jcn - Wolverhampton - Coseley - Tipton - Spon Lane - Soho - Gas Street Basin
Worcester and Birmingham Canal (1815)
  Gas Street Basin - King's Norton Junction - Tardebigge - Hanbury Jcn - Diglis Basins
Severn Navigation (1812, 1842)
  Worcester - Stourport
Staffordshire and Worcestershire Canal (1772)
  Stourport - Kidderminster - Cookley - Kinver - Stourton - Botterham - The Bratch - Aldersley Jcn

Allow 50 hours travelling.
65 miles of narrow canal, 13 miles of river, 8 tunnels, 119 narrow locks, 3 wide locks.

Drop down from the Birminham plateau through the longest lock flight, test the waters of the River Severn, climb gently up the attractive Stour Valley. Plenty to see in Worcester and Birmingham.

Visitor attractions

Black Country Living Museum
Period dress, old money, tram rides. Vast collection of real buildings brought together into a village after being dismantled from redevelopment sites all over the Black Country. Seek out lime kilns to see huge scale of Lord Ward's industrial operation (1778). No wonder the woods above are pockmarked like a WWI battlefield.
Tie up actually in the museum itself.
Brindley Place
Heart of Birmingham with restaurants, bars, cafés, museums, theatres, galleries and huge pedestrian shopping areas.
Tie up near Broad Street Bridge.
Cadbury World (Tel:0121 451 4180)
Chocolate makers fantastic fantasy. Great trip for the kids. Tells the story of how we came to eat so much and how Coronation Street got involved. Sadly does not relate Cadbury's long association with canals (1915-1930, 1966-1968). Regular runs in distinctive livery to Liverpool for sugar, to Cheshire for milk and to deliver cocoa and chocolate to London.
Tie up near Bridge 77.
Avoncroft Museum of Historic Buildings
Three-seater earth closet from Leominster is the smallest of the rescued and rebuilt structures. Others include local nail works, working windmill, timber-framed houses and the Guesten Hall roof from Worcester Cathedral Priory sitting on a new hall. UK Telephone Koisk Collection. (Tel: 01527 831363)
Tie up at Stoke Wharf or Bridge 48. Walk north.
The Commandery, Worcester
War Rooms of Charles II prior to battle (1651).
Tie up above Sidbury Lock 3, alongside the entrance.
Severn Valley Steam Railway (Tel: 01299 403816)
Upstream beyond the current limit of navigation to Bewdley, Hampton Loade ferry and Bridgenorth. 16 mile railway that may go to Ironbridge one day.
Tie up in Kidderminster above Lock 6. Cross the highway into town and beyond to Railtrack's station.
Kinver Edge
Wooded ridge with magnificent views, popular with

Birmingham people since Victorian times.
Tie up above Kinver Lock.

Waterway distractions

Wolverhampton Lock Flight
21 locks in a mile and half. The Birmingham Canal Company's finale (1772), linking the plateau to the wider canal network for the first time. Passes Racecourse and ends amid a rural cutting.

Gas Street Basin
Worcester and Birmingham Canal's 20 year stand-off with the Birmingham Canal Company meant double handling across the 7 foot Worcester Bar. Today's attractions are pubs and clubs clustered around the heart of the canal system. Flood-lit towpaths at night.
Tie up for an afternoon and walk the towpaths.

Tardebigge Locks
Thirty locks climbing 217 feet plus the six at Stoke - provides a baptism of fire - 36 locks in four miles. The top lock might have been a small boat lift, but the failed experiment has left us with a 14 foot chamber.

Aickman - Rolt Plaque
The top lock of the flight was practically in the middle of nowhere when Robert Aickman walked from Bromsgrove station to meet his fellow author Tom Rolt, living here with his wife Angela on their narrowboat 'Cressy' (1946). This historic meeting led to the founding of the Inland Waterways Association which campaigned for over 50 years for Governments to recognise all inland waterways as an asset not a liability. Present Government now accepts this view and encourages everyone to use the water, hedgerows and towing paths for the recreational opportunities they offer.
IWA commemorative plaque tells the story by Lock 1.

Bittell Reservoirs (1815, 1832)
Lower Bittell Reservoir was provided solely for millers on the Rea and Arrow Rivers downstream. Upper Bittell feeds the canal itself.
Tie up near Bridges 65 or 66. Short walk north.

Stourport Basins
Two sets of narrow staircase locks and two vast 'barge' locks sized for Severn Trows lead from the

Wooded Kinver Edge

variable levels of the River Severn into the calm of two large basins. Two major commercial buildings complete the picture - The Tontine Hotel built for passengers and the Clock Warehouse built for goods.
Tie up just outside the basin, but give them a whirl.

The Bratch (30 feet) (3 locks)
Much photographed locks and octagonal toll office, generally supported by groups of gongoozlers, Locks are apparently close enough to be a staircase, but actually work by disposing of the water through swirling culverts to hidden pounds to one side.
Take instructions from the lock keeper.

Aldersley and Autherley Junctions
A pair of turnings off one of the oldest canals in the country (1772), one climbs up to Birmingham (1772), the other is the start of Telford's straight-as-a-die link to Liverpool (1835).
See remains of toll keepers' cottages and stables.

Short cut
Climb up to the Birmingham plateau by the route Lord Dudley intended. Turn right at Stourton Junction into the Stourbridge Canal, past the Town Arm to Parkhead. Then through the wide towpath-lined Netherton Tunnel (9080 feet) to Dudley Port Junction.
13 miles, 29 locks. Allow 11 hours. 9 miles and 11 locks less, thus saving 5 hours.

Worth a detour
Lapworth Locks
Lock-free run to the top of a flight of 26 locks.
10½ miles, 0 locks each way. Allow 6 hours.

Tewkesbury
Run down to the River Avon, past Upton upon Severn.
16 miles, 1 lock each way. Allow 9 hours.

i *Tourist Information*
Wolverhampton Tel: 01902 312051
Dudley Tel: 01384 812830
Birmingham Tel: 0121 693 6300
Worcester Tel: 01905 726311
Kidderminster Tel: 01562 829400

Cruising Maps
GEOprojects: *Staffordshire and Worcestershire Canal with the River Severn and the Gloucester and Sharpness Canal*
GEOprojects: *Worcester and Birmingham Canal with the Droitwich Canals*
GEOprojects: *Birmingham Canal Navigations*

Start Points

5	Alvechurch Boat Centres	**66**	Evesham Marina Holidays
18	Anglo Welsh Waterway Holidays	**93**	Pegary Boat Hire
21	Anglo Welsh Waterway Holidays	**105**	Sherborne Wharf
31	Bidford Boats	**109**	Starline Narrowboats
36	Black Prince Holidays	**110**	Stroudwater Cruisers
44	Brook Line Narrowboat Holidays	**115**	Telstar Cruisers Ltd
60	Copt Heath Wharf	**119**	Viking Afloat
63	Countrywide Cruisers	**122**	Viking Afloat
		124	Water Travel Ltd

James Brindley, Gas Street Basin, Birmingham

Kennet and Avon Canal

Lush valley, unspoilt villages, dramatic gorge.

Tidal Avon Navigation (1727)
Floating Harbour (1809) - Netham - Hanham
Kennet and Avon Canal - West (1810)
Hanham - Widcombe Flight - Claverton - Dundas - Avoncliff - Bradford-on-Avon - Semington - Seend Locks - Caen Hill Lock Flight
Kennet and Avon Canal - East (1799)
Caen Hill Lock Flight - Devizes - Long pound - Pewsey - Bruce Tunnel - Crofton - Hungerford - Kintbury - Newbury Wharf
River Kennet Navigation (1724)
Newbury Wharf - Monkey Marsh - Aldermaston - High Bridge, Reading - Blake's Lock - Kennet Mouth on the Thames

Allow 55 hours travelling end to end. The canal is not part of a ring, so all hirings require a return to home base (thus minimum 110 hours travelling). A holiday covering the whole canal involves two energetic crossings of the Caen Hill Lock Flight which alone can take up to 5 hours to negotiate, thereby creating a canal of two halves.
West: 14 miles of river, 22 miles of wide canal.
2 aqueducts, 29 locks and 9 swing bridges.
Caen Hill Flight: 16 locks in one mile.
East: 18 miles of river, 34 miles of wide canal.
1 tunnel, 63 locks and 17 swing bridges.

The canal climbs steadily away from the Thames, up a pastoral valley playing 'Cox and Box' with the River Kennet. A short tunnel stands in the two pounds between Devizes and Clifton and after the steep Caen Hill Lock Flight, a lock free Avon Gorge leads to the 'World Heritage' City of Bath. This wide waterway connecting to the Severn Estuary was the subject of a long campaign for restoration (1955-1965-1990), finally completed with the help of Lottery funds (1996-2002).

Visitor attractions

Bristol
Harveys Wine Cellars, Arnofini Centre, Bristol Blue Glass makers, Harbour Railway all lie close to the Harbour. Zoo Gardens and Clifton Suspension Bridge Visitor Centre are a taxi ride away.
Tie up in the Floating Harbour.
SS Great Britain (1843, 1970) (Tel: 0117 926 0680)
Isambard Kingdom Brunel designed three huge steamships. Wrought iron plates were made in Coalbrookdale and shipped down the Severn to this very dock to be shaped and riveted into the world's first luxury passenger liner powered by propellers and the biggest steam engine of its time.
Tie up in the Floating Harbour.
Pulteney Weir, Bath
Elegant, curved, stepped weir is limit of navigation. Still water mirrors Robert Adam's famous bridge.
Tie up on superb visitor moorings short of weir.
Visit 'World Heritage' City of Bath.
Roman Baths (Tel: 01225 477785)
Aquae Sulis. Site of healing natural hot springs held in religious awe since Celtic times (a million litres per day at 42°C). Temple of Sulis Minerva.
Tie up just short of the weir. Cross by North Parade.
American Museum, Claverton Manor
Decorative arts from across the pond (1650-1850).
Tie up at Bridge 179.
Great Tithe Barn, Bradford-on-Avon
Granary for Shaftesbury Abbey which collected one tenth of all local produce. Rich pickings! Stone walls, 168 feet long beamed roof (Tel: 01225 865797).
Tie up above Lock 14.
Devizes Wharf
Restored Town Wharf. Waterfront warehouse is a theatre. The long warehouse contains the Kennet and Avon Canal Trust's museum which tells the story of the canal from 1794 to date. Start of the Easter Canoe Challenge to Westminster - 125 miles and 77 locks.
Tie up at the wharf.
Vale of Pewsey
Downland Wiltshire - Neolithic camps, long barrows and Pewsey Downs Nature Reserve. Pewsey Heritage Centre in a former foundry building.

The Victorian Boating Station, Bath

Tie up near Bridges 114, 124, 125, 126 or 127.
Savernake Forest
2000 acres of ancient hunting forest. Unbroken woodland enmeshed with many paths and rides. Beech, chestnut, oak and newer plantings surround the long walk to Marlborough. Red and fallow deer.
Tie up at the western portal of Bruce Tunnel.
Hungerford Common
Many commons around the country have since been enclosed. This is still held by the local citizens and provides easy walks across rough grazing.
Tie up near Lock 75.
Theale Lakes: Lower Kennet Water Park
Former gravel workings now nature reserves, osier beds and lakes for sailing, wind surfing, water skiing.
Tie up near Bridges 14, 15, 17 or 19.
Oracle Shopping Centre, Reading
Modern centre includes cinemas, cafés and clubs either side of a sometimes fast flowing river.
Tie up on the Abbey backwater. Walk around.
Blake's Lock Museum
Bakery, gentlemen's hairdresser, printer's workshop from the 19th Century are reconstructed as part of a museum celebrating Reading's Victorian industries. Waterways displays. Restored gypsy ledge caravan.
Tie up short of Blake's Lock.

Waterway distractions

Floating Harbour, Bristol
A harbour where boats were always floating - so much better than being stranded on the riverbed by the retreating 40 foot tide.
Tie up in the harbour.

Widcombe Locks 7-13, Bath
Final drop into the river from the 9 miles of contour hugging pound from Bradford-on-Avon. Two steam driven back pumps were installed to recover used water. Chimney stacks remain at Locks 7 and 11.
Tie up at the top lock.

Claverton Pumping Station
Ecologically sound engineering, taking water from the river to supply the canal 47 feet above.
Tie up near Bridge 179. Open summer Sundays.

Dundas Aqueduct (1805, 1984)
Dramatic setting for a dogleg crossing of the river, Rennie's magnificent architecture at the junction with the now closed Somersetshire Coal Canal.
Tie up short. Walk around.

Avoncliff Aqueduct
Higher and longer than Dundas. Best viewed from the river bank below.
Tie up at moorings on the west side.

Wilts and Berks Canal
Narrow canal once led off towards the Thames and Severn Canal at Cricklade and the Thames itself at Abingdon. Still visible for the most part. Some new lengths needed to bypass recent urban developments. A Canal Partnership is on the case.
Stop at Lock 15. Old line went north alongside road.

Caen Hill Flight (130 feet) (1810, 1990)
Central spectacular feature of the canal, sixteen locks in close succession with seriously large side pounds which even out water levels. Much photographed.
Lock keeper assisted passage. (Tel: 01380 722859).

Crofton Pumping Station (Tel: 01672 870300)
Two huge steam engines are reactivated once a month in summer. Water is drawn from Wilton Water under the canal and then lifted 40 feet to the level of a leat which runs back to the summit pound. One ton at a time, every five seconds. Mind blowing.
Tie up below Lock 60.

Replica of John Cabot's Caravel 'The Matthew' (1497) and SS Great Britain (1843), Floating Harbour, Bristol

Monkey Marsh Lock
Turf-sided lock, as were all original locks of the Kennet Navigation. Cheaper to build, water filled an ever widening chamber - a huge volume with each passing boat. Scheduled Ancient Monument.
Tie up before the lock. Walk around.

Aldermaston Wharf (Tel: 0118 971 2868)
Visitor Centre near railway station with picnic area. Discovery Trails into the surrounding countryside.
Tie up at the wharf. Lift bridge fixed at peak times.

ℹ️ Tourist Information
Bristol Tel: 0117 926 0767
Bath Tel: 01225 477000
Devizes Tel: 01380 729408
Marlborough Tel: 01672 513989
Newbury Tel: 01635 30267
Reading Tel: 0118 956 6226

📖 Suggested Guide Book
Niall Allsop *The Kennet and Avon Canal* Millstream Books, 1992

Cruising Maps
GEOprojects: Kennet and Avon Canal

Start Points
11 Anglo Welsh Waterway Holidays	**45** Foxhangers Canal Holidays
12 Anglo Welsh Waterway Holidays	**46** Bruce Charitable Trust
30 Berry Brook Boats	**81** Kennet Cruises
30 London & Home Counties Narrowboat Holidays	**87** Moonraker Narrowboats
	87 Wessex Narrowboats
39 Bridge Boats Ltd	**95** Reading Marine Co
39 Caversham Boat Services	**102** Sally Boats
45 Bruce Charitable Trust	**111** Sunset Holidays
	128 White Horse Boats

Warwickshire Ring

Lots of locks and lots of lock-free miles.

Coventry Canal (1790)
  Fazeley Jcn - Atherstone - Marston Jcn -
  Hawkesbury Jcn
Oxford Canal (1774, 1834)
  Hawkesbury Jcn - Newbold - Hillmorton -
  Braunston - Napton Jcn
Grand Union Canal (1779, 1935)
  Napton Jcn - Stockton - Hatton - Shrewley -
  Kingswood Jcn - Knowle - Typhoo Basin
Birmingham and Fazeley Canal (1789)
  Typhoo Basin - Ashted - Aston - Salford Jcn -
  Curdworth - Fazeley Jcn

Allow 50 hours travelling.
59 miles of narrow canal, 39 miles of wide canal, 3
tunnels, 6 aqueducts, 43 narrow locks, 47 wide locks.

Visit Warwick, Coventry, Royal Leamington Spa
from a ring that is mostly fields and meadows.

Visitor attractions

Brinklow Castle
Once a major protection for Fosse Way, grassed
motte and bailey is preserved in fields.
From Bridge 34 go towards Brinklow, turn left at the
T-junction and walk up the hill. Wide main street.
Rugby School (Tel: 01788 542426)
William Webb Ellis picked up the ball and ran with it -
inventing Rugby Football. See Gilbert Museum.
Tie up near picnic site. Longer walk to town centre.
Napton Windmill
Landmark-on-the-hill. Long views of Warwickshire.
Stop near Bridge 111. Climb by field hedges to
village.
Welsh Road
Not Roman, but a long, wide, drovers' route that
followed the Iron Age Jurassic Way and brought
sheep and tar-footed geese to London's population.
Diverted by the canal company into a dogleg over
Bridge 30.
Royal Pump Room
Set amid Jephson Gardens with the River Avon
flowing through.
Tie up near Bridge 40. Walk, past modest railway

Moira Furnace

Braunston Marina, Grand Union Canal

housing, under the railway bridge to cross the River
Avon bridge.
Warwick Castle
Great Hall, state rooms, ghost tower, armoury,
dungeon and torture chamber, All behind ramparts
that are largely unchanged and overlook the River
Avon.
Tie up near the Avon Aqueduct. Go down the steps to
follow the riverbank into town.
Kingsbury Water Park (Tel: 01827 872660)
20 lakes harbouring wildlife, twitchers, picnicers,
walkers, plus paddling and adventurous children.
Tie up at Bodymoor Heath Bridge.
Drayton Manor Family Theme Park
Animals, gentle kids stuff and white knuckle thrills -
into water and a 160 foot drop into a void - haunting.
Tie up at Coleshill Road Bridge, just opposite.

Waterway distractions

Fazeley Junction
Lines of both canals set to give access to Watling
Street and Turnpike (A5). Original 'Arkwright' Mill
three storeys, 19 bays and a water system to power it.
Tie up near junction. Cross Tolson's Footbridge.
Griff Arm at Newdigate Colliery
Considering Sir Richard promoted both the Coventry
and Oxford Canals, the waterway entrance to his
colliery arm is surprisingly low.
Note the sharp corner at Bridge 13.
Sutton Stop at Hawkesbury
Mr Sutton checked the boats coming through the
Stop Lock onto the Oxford Canal. The Engine House
(1821) gained an early Newcomen Engine after 100
years working at Griff Colliery nearby and then lost it
to Darmouth - Newcomen's birthplace (1963).
Tie up on visitor moorings. See the improved garden.
Newbold Old Tunnel (1774)
Portal of this tunnel can be seen in the churchyard.
Replaced by wide tunnel with twin towpaths (1834).
Tie up near Bridge 50. Village lane crosses over.
Hillmorton Paired Locks (1840)
Only locks on the North Oxford Canal, duplicated to
speed up passage when the line was straightened.
Use either lock depending on which is set for you.
Braunston Turn
When the North Oxford Canal was shortened by 33%
(1834), towpath bridges from Horseley Iron Works
were standard issue. Seen here - and all points north.

Tie up on the embankment. Walk back to the village.
Stockton Lock Flight
Flight that rises through the tree covered abandoned
workings of Blue Lias stone which contained fossils
from the Jurassic period.
New locks (1934) match those on Grand Union Canal
(1800).
Hatton Lock Flight (146 feet) (21 wide locks)
Spectacular rise through a wide fairway that includes
the site of the former narrow locks. Distinctive pods
alongside the locks enclose worm gearing to raise the
ground paddles.
Tie up at the top, look back over Warwick.
Shrewley Tunnel
Actually two. One for boats and one for horses.
Maybe drop off a crew member to walk the towpath.
Fellows, Moreton and Clayton (1837-1949)
Next to Typhoo Basin, one of many warehouses for
general merchandise and foodstuffs owned by this
pro-active carrying firm. They pioneered 'steamers'
once owning 21 in their 208 boat fleet (1920). They
pressured canal companies for improvements - the
Grand Union Canal (1894), Warwick Canals (1903) -
and for wider locks at Foxton and Watford on the
Leicester Line.
Tie up near Warwick Bar - the neck in the canal acted
as a control for payment of canal dues. Other
canalside features have also been retained.
Salford Junction
Crazy memorial to centuries of engineering. A river
bridged by a road (since 1290). Two canals make a
junction and bridge over the river (1789). Over the
top of the lot, see the many levels of bridges erected
to cope with the needs of speeding road vehicles - the
Spaghetti Junction slip roads for M6 / A38(M).
Tie up, look up, avoid the drips.

Worth a detour

Fradley Junction
Pop up to the older Trent and Mersey Canal and have
a drink at the white painted 'Swan', a boatman's pub.
7 miles, 0 locks each way. Allow 5 hours.
Bosworth Field and Moira Furnace
Lock-free through rolling country to a famous battle
and beyond to Snarestone. Until the restoration gets
there take a taxi to Moira Furnace and Heart of the
National Forest Centre nearby (Tel: 01283 224667).
22 miles, 0 locks each way. Allow 15 hours plus taxi.

Bishop Street Basin, Coventry
Five miles of canalside artworks adorn a much improved approach to Lady Godiva's City.
5¼ miles, 0 locks each way. Allow 3 hours.
Birmingham Bright Lights: Brindley Place
Restaurants, bars, bistros and cafés abound. Water buses, trip boats. Sea Life Centre and National Indoor Arena - International Conference Centre with Birmingham Symphony Orchestra.

3 miles, 13 locks at Farmer's Bridge each way. Allow 8 hours, or walk the towpath and only allow 2 hours.
Crick and Welford Arm
Through Braunston Tunnel onto the Old Grand Union Canal. Built with wide bridges and tunnels (1814), this link to wide canals at Foxton and Market Harborough was let down by its narrow locks. Go through Watford Locks (includes a four-lock staircase with large side pounds) and Crick Tunnel. Gentle village. Reservoirs.

22 miles, 14 locks each way. Allow 19 hours.
Bancroft Basin, Stratford
Down a delightful valley to Shakespeare Country.
14 miles, 38 locks each way. Allow 22 hours.

ℹ️ *Tourist Information*
Tamworth Tel: 01827 59134
Nuneaton Tel: 01203 347006
Coventry Tel: 01230 832304
Rugby Tel: 01788 571813
Royal Leamington Spa Tel: 01926 881639
Warwick Tel: 01926 492212
Birmingham Tel: 0121 693 6300

GEO *Cruising Maps*
GEOprojects: *Coventry and Ashby Canals and the Birmingham and Fazeley Canal*
GEOprojects: *Oxford Canal*
GEOprojects: *Grand Union Canal map 1, Birmingham to Fenny Stratford*
GEOprojects: *Grand Union Canal map 4, Leicester Line, Soar Navigation and Erewash Canal*
GEOprojects: *Birmingham Canal Navigations*
GEOprojects: *Stratford-upon-Avon Canal and the River Avon (2002)*

Start Points

21 Anglo Welsh Waterway Holidays	88 Napton Narrowboats
23 Ashby Boat Company	93 Pegary Boat Hire
47 Calcutt Boats Ltd	100 Rose Narrowboats Ltd
50 Canalboat Holidays Ltd	105 Sherborne Wharf
56 Clifton Cruisers	113 Swan Line Cruisers Ltd
57 Club Line Cruisers	117 Union Canal Carriers Ltd
57 London & Home Counties Narrowboat Holidays	118 Valley Cruises Ltd
	120 Viking Afloat
60 Copt Heath Wharf	120 Willow Wren Cruising Holidays
61 Coronet Canal Carrying Co	
80 Kate Boats Warwick	125 Weltonfield Narrowboats Ltd

More time

Once you have caught the bug, the prospect of spending more time on the water beckons. Some equip their boats with extra modern conveniences - dishwashers, washing machines, sound systems, e-mail capabilities - and then proceed to spend a whole summer away from home. We have met Americans, Australians and Scandinavians who have their own boats and do this every year. There is also an increasing number of British couples who emulate them, even staying on the water all through the winter. Some set themselves the task of covering the whole system, including all the river navigations to York and back, which is just about feasible if you have already retired and have two or more years to spare.

Most people hiring a boat might limit themselves to a maximum of three or four weeks and be prepared to indulge themselves in all the 'messing about on the water' that this allows. The four suggestions that follow are only a few of the journeys that are possible, but it makes a start.

Four Counties Ring

Salt, Potteries and the Cheshire Plain.

Shropshire Union Canal - Middlewich Branch (1834)
   Barbridge Jcn - Weaver Aqueduct - Wardle Lock
Wardle Canal (300 feet) (1833)
   Wardle Lock - Middlewich Jcn
Trent and Mersey Canal (1777)
   Middlewich Jcn - Hardings Wood Jcn - Harecastle - Etruria Jcn - Stone - Great Haywood Jcn
Staffordshire and Worcestershire Canal (1772)
   Great Haywood Jcn - Hatherton Jcn - Autherley Jcn
Shropshire Union Canal - Main Line, (1835)
   Autherley Jcn - Stretton Aqueduct - Norbury - Shebdon - Tyrley - Audlem - Nantwich - Hurleston Jcn - Barbridge Jcn

Allow 55 hours travelling on the ring itself plus extra hours if you choose to detour.
14 miles of wide canal, 96 miles of narrow canal,
1 tunnel, 9 aqueducts, 4 embankments, 4 wide locks,
90 narrow locks.

Admittedly you do not need extra time to complete this ring. Some even manage to finish it in a good week's boating, but these waterways provide an unusual approach to the remote farmlands and rural pastimes of the Cheshire Plain and are best savoured slowly.

The canals take an independent line past Market Drayton and Audlem, so independent that only country lanes cross the canal, only pastoral scenes line its banks. On the edge of the Plain, as you climb the locks of Heartbreak Hill the whole panorama is laid out before you.

The ring has much of waterways interest including two early canals and Telford's final fling from Birmingham to Nantwich. There are three convenient detours which extend the experience and during 2002 the restored Anderton Lift will add access to the slow, wide River Weaver Navigation.

Visitor attractions

Sandbach Saxon Crosses
Two stone crosses, erected in 1600s, broken and dispersed to the four winds by Puritans. Many pieces identified and gathered in by George Ormerod who re-erected them in the market square (1816).
Tie up near Bridge 151 or 154.

Westport Lake Park
Circular lakeside walk alongside the canal.
Tie up near Bridge 128.

Festival Park
Early National Garden Festival (1986) transformed a redundant steelworks site, now home to multi-cinema complex, fast food restaurants and a supermarket. Josiah Wedgwood's private residence, Etruria Hall, is now restored as part of the Moat House Hotel.
Tie up near Festival Park Marina.

Etruria Bone and Flint Mill
Now part of the modern Etruria Industrial Museum, Jesse Shirley's Bone and Flint Mill (1857-1972) had 12 grinding pans each driven through sets of gears from a single beam steam engine 'Princess'(1822).

Flints and bones were brought by canal and product sent all over the Potteries. Engine regularly in steam.
Tie up in the wide basin before the new entrance.

Factory Tours: Potteries
Factories of Royal Doulton at Burslem and Spode at Stoke plus Gladstone Working Pottery Museum at Longton all provide some hands-on experience of creative use of clay and the potters wheel. A 'China Link Bus' connects these and other attractions.
(Tel: 01782 319232)
Tie up near Bridge 118. Walk north or catch a local bus to Hanley Bus Station.

Trentham Gardens (Tel: 01782 657341)
Ballroom and Orangery survive the demolition of the Hall (1909). Italianate gardens contain boating lake, swimming pool and miniature railway.
Tie up at Bridge 106.

Wedgwood Potteries: Barlaston
Transferred onto this greenfield site from the original factory close to Etruria Junction (1940), the factory was a pioneer in the use of smoke-free electric ovens. With a factory shop, demonstations and an exhibition of all its designs, this is unmissable for some.
Tie up near Bridge 104. Walk along country lanes.

Shugborough Hall (Tel: 01889 881388)
Lord Lichfield, photographer, is only the latest in a line of Astons who have created the Mansion House. Financed by Spanish gold, the estate has monuments and follies of Roman, Greek and Oriental inspiration. Servants quarters, laundry, brewhouse, butler's pantry great kitchen, scullery, carriage houses and stables are the basis of Staffordshire County's 'Museum of Staffordshire Life'.
Stop short of Bridge 74. Use the towpath to Haywood Lock. Use the Packhorse Bridge over the River Trent.

Stafford County Town
Star of the 'Town Trail' is The Ancient High House (1595), a massive Tudor timber-framed town house, largest in England. Herb garden, Shire Hall Gallery, once the Crown Court, Victorian Park, mill pond.
Tie up near Radford Bridge 98. Enter over Green Bridge (1285) site of original ford. 2 mile walk.

Brewood
Delightful village stands above the cutting. Small specialist shops and hostelries.
Tie up near Bridge 14.

Cowley
Seriously steep-sided cuttings end in a short tunnel carved through raw rock. The resulting micro-climate encourages all kinds of fern and lichen and a slippery towpath.
Tie up near Bridge 34.

Nantwich
Roman 'wich' or saltmaking town. Devastated by fire (1583), rebuilt in half-timbered Tudor construction. Many buildings still surviving.
Tie up at south of the aqueduct. Walk into town.

Leaving Tixall Wide

Talke o' the Hill

An early road from Poynton and Congleton joined the early waggoners route to London, Holyhead and Carlisle. Here Matthew Pickford met his wife Hannah Taylor and they later added carrying services on canals to their waggoning business - owning ten boats in 1795.
Tie up at Bridge 130. Cross over the tunnel mouth and a long walk southwest.

Waterway distractions

Heartbreak Hill

26 locks in seven miles lift the canal 250 feet above the Cheshire Plain. Most were duplicated (1830) and allow simultaneously traffic both up and down. Banks are reinforced against the threat of further salt mining subsidence.

Thurlwood Steel Lock

Guillotine gates to a steel tank replacing one of the twin locks collapsing due to subsidence. They took longer to operate and were eventually removed (1987).
Tie up near Lock 53. See the interpretation board.

Red Bull Aqueduct

A bold stone waterway slip road. The route to Macclesfield crosses the Trent and Mersey Canal here having made the at-grade 'turn off' ½ mile and two locks to the south.
Tie up between Locks 41 and 42. Walk the two towpaths.

Harecastle Tunnels (8778 feet)

James Brindley's original tunnel (1777) was started seven years before and finished five years after he died. It was the only route for 50 years and became a serious bottleneck. A second tunnel (Telford 1827) was completed in three years creating a sort of dual-carriageway of the waterways. Now with towpath removed and substantially improved it is the only way through. The tunnel has a massive door that closes behind you to allow the huge fans to ventilate.
Arrive between 8am and 3pm. Saturdays only in
winter. Tie up and wait for the tunnel keeper to log your name and number. Crew can walk over the top if they wish.

Great Haywood Junction Bridge

Subject of a famous illustration (62) in Eric de Maré's seminal book 'The Canals of England', published (1950) as a special number of The Architectural Review. A 'strange, remote, unearthly atmosphere'.
Tie up short of the busy junction.

Tixall Wide

An appeasement of the local gentry, willing to tolerate the canal provided it didn't spoil the view from the hall. The canal becomes a wide lake with wildlife galore and the noisy railway is silenced by entering a tunnel to the south.
Tie up along the towpath. Idyllic overnight moorings.

Gailey Round House

Toll keeper's watch tower. Now a canal shop.
Alongside Lock 32 in small canal settlement.

Hatherton Junction

Place name came after this junction was created. Named after a Chairman of the Board. One lock on the branch is in use as a dry dock.
Tie up, walk over the bridge.

Twin Junctions: Autherley and Aldersley

Short water in rural cutting joins two canals.
Stop at bottom of Wolverhampton Lock Flight. Look around.

Pendeford Rockin

Sandstone outcrop that challenged Brindley (1772). Cut with pickaxe, the result is narrower than most sections.
Take care in the passing bays.

Stretton Aqueduct

Early Telford appointments were Surveyor of Public Works to County of Salop and consultant to the Holyhead Road (A5). When his last canal design passed over the A5 he celebrated in ornate cast iron.
Tie up short. Walk down to the roadside.

Shelmore Embankment (1 mile long, 60 feet high)

Diverted from the straight line by his Lordship, this was a constant worry to an ailing Telford. The earth from nearby cuttings refused to remain stable and was constantly slipping. Now secure, it was only completed 12 months after the rest was ready.
Tie up on the 48 hour visitor moorings. Walk around.

Norbury Junction

Former branch of the Shrewsbury and Newport Canal, built to connect the new (1835) canal to the earlier system around Ironbridge (1792) which for many years had connected coal mines at Ketley and Donnington Wood and furnaces at Blist Hill and Coalbrookdale - the Shropshire Canal.
Start of lock flight is now used by boatyard.

Cadbury's Wharf and Factory

No longer scene of milk churns being delivered by day-boats or raw chocolate on its way to Bourneville.
Tie up. See warehouse canopy and ex-working boat.

Woodseaves Cutting

Long (4500 feet) narrow, steep sided and deep (100 feet), sometimes cut in raw red sandstone rock. The microclimate nurtures ferns and a slippery towpath.
Beyond the top of Tyrley Locks.

Tyrley Locks

Arched over by trees in the countryside south of Market Drayton. One of only three flights of locks on Telford's Birmingham and Liverpool Junction Canal.
Tie up at Tyrley Wharf.

Audlem Locks and Wharf

The wharf is near the bottom of the 15 lock flight. Warehouse with its crane now serves ale, and the Old Mill serves boater's needs. Little shops supply everything else, including trainers in the Post Office. Daystar Theatre Group in the stables at the bottom.
Tie up at the wharf.

Nantwich Basin

Terminus of the older wide Chester Canal to Ellesmere Port. Telford's arrow-straight narrow Birmingham and Liverpool Junction Canal takes off from just outside the basin.
Take care. They join on a tight angle.

Hurleston Reservoir

85,000,000 gallons reserved to support the canal and subsequently for the citizens of Nantwich and Crewe. Supplied from the River Dee at Horseshoe Falls by millions of gallons a day flowing down the canal. This secondary purpose ensured the canal was maintained and never filled in during the 'dark days'.
Tie up at the bottom of the four lock flight.

Twin Junctions: Hurleston and Barbridge

Two narrow turnings off the older, wider Chester Canal lead to Llangollen Canal and the Four Counties Ring respectively.
Busy on summer weekends.

Winsford Flashes

Lakes created by salt mining subsidence, filled by River Weaver waters. Ignominious graveyard of many working boats when the British Transport Commission decided that carrying was uneconomic.
Tie up at Bridge 22. Look down the valley.

Wardle Canal (600 feet and one lock)

Probably the shortest canal on the system joining the wide beam Middlewich Branch of the (then) Chester Canal to the Trent and Mersey Canal. The Duke of Bridgewater was a major influence on the committee of the Trent and Mersey Canal and when the Chester Canal was first promoted (1771) he objected, forcing them to agree never to come within 100 yards of the

Tyrley Top Lock

Trent and Mersey Canal. 44 years later when Telford proposed a new canal direct from Birmingham to Nantwich, the Trent and Mersey Canal relented and agreed to a connection at Middlewich, therefore giving itself access to the new route to Birmingham. These last few yards at Middlewich were financed by the Trent and Mersey Canal, but were called by a different name. The Chester Canal has therefore never come closer than 100 yards of the Trent and Mersey Canal.

See the key stone on the road Bridge 168.

Worth a detour

Wrenbury Mill
Up the first locks of the Llangollen Canal.
6 miles, 9 locks each way. Allow 8 hours.

Bosley Locks
One stop lock and lock free to the River Dane.
10 miles, 1 lock each way. Allow 6 hours.

Chester
Past Beeston Castle to the Roman Port. Cathedral, complete city walls, Taylors Yard.
16 miles wide canal, 14 locks each way. Allow 16 hours.

Weaver Navigation (1732) **via Anderton Lift** (2002)
Wide river, weirs, water meadows and sea going craft.
20 miles, 4 huge locks each way. Allow 6 hours plus your scheduled time through Anderton Lift (booking essential - fee).

ℹ️ *Tourist Information*
Congleton Tel: 01260 271095
Stoke-on-Trent Tel: 01782 284600
Newcastle-under-Lyme Tel: 01782 297313
Wolverhampton Tel: 01902 312051
Stafford Tel: 01785 240204
Market Drayton Tel: 01630 652139
Nantwich Tel: 01270 610983
Cheshire Tourism Tel: 01244 603127
Chester Tel: 01244 322220

🗺️ *Cruising Maps*
GEOprojects: *Trent and Mersey Canal map 1, Preston Brook to Fradley Junction*
GEOprojects: *Shropshire Union Canal*
GEOprojects: *Staffordshire and Worcestershire Canal with the River Severn and the Gloucester and Sharpness Canal*
GEOprojects: *Macclesfield and Peak Forest Canals with the Ashton Canal*
GEOprojects: *Llangollen and Montgomery Canals*

Start Points

7	Alvechurch Boat Centres	**53**	Chas. Hardern & Co
8	Alvechurch Boat Centres	**54**	Cheshire Cat
10	Andersen Boats		Narrowboat Hire
10	Middlewich Narrowboats	**55**	Claymoore Navigation
13	Anglo Welsh		Ltd
	Waterway Holidays	**59**	Constellation Cruises Ltd
14	Anglo Welsh	**63**	Countrywide Cruisers
	Waterway Holidays	**65**	Empress Holidays Ltd
16	Anglo Welsh	**77**	Heritage Narrowboats
	Waterway Holidays	**92**	Peak Forest Cruisers
17	Anglo Welsh	**114**	Teddesley Boat Company
	Waterway Holidays	**119**	Viking Afloat
32	Black Prince Holidays	**121**	Viking Afloat
35	Black Prince Holidays	**124**	Water Travel Ltd
51	Canal Cruising		
	Company Ltd		

Anderton Lift before restoration

Anderton Lift (1875-1956, 2002)

On the opening of the Trent and Mersey Canal, the Weaver Navigation built a basin under the cliff where the canal passed close to the river at Anderton. For 80 years they attracted increasing trade through the salt rushing down wooden chutes to land in special Weaver Flats which then delivered the salt further downstream.

Engineer to the Navigation, Edward Leader Williams, then commissioned a design for the world's first boat lift from Edwin Clark (completed 1875). The design consisted of two huge (250 ton) caissons each sitting on a hydraulic ram. These were linked so that the descending tank forced the ram under the second tank to lift it by the same amount. Thus counterbalanced the steam energy required to activate the lift was minimal.

After only seven years (1882) one of the rams burst. It took 6 months to repair and 20 years later (1905) inspection indicated that corrosion had attacked both rams. Rather than stop the lift for significant repairs, a radical change was implemented. The completely new system involved independent counterbalancing weights (totaling 250 tons each set) attached to each caisson and driven by independent electric motors. This was constructed on a huge new frame around the existing structure whilst the lift was still operating. The operational changeover was accomplished during one Bank Holiday weekend.

The result was a new structure dominated by two sets of six foot diameter pulleys at the top, which fed the ropes from the counterweights to the cassions.

The restoration project has returned to the original design with modern rams and modern hydraulics. The pulleys are still on site but no longer take an active part in the lifting process. Look in the tents.

Passage is available to boats and pedestrians for a small fee. Legal ownership is by the Waterways Trust on behalf of an array of organisations who have funded the restoration. (Tel: 0151 355 5017)
www.andertonboatlift.co.uk

Thames Ring
Royal river and two canals.

Tidal River Thames
  Brentford - Richmond Lock - Teddington Locks
Lower River Thames
  Teddington Locks - Shepperton - Staines - Windsor -
  Henley - Reading - Goring - Wallingford -
  Abingdon - Isis Lock, Oxford
Oxford Canal (1790)
  Isis Lock - Duke's Cut - Aynho - Banbury -
  Fenny Compton - Napton Jcn - Braunston Turn
Grand Union Canal (1800, 1929)
  Braunston Turn - Norton Jcn - Gayton Jcn -
  Blisworth - Cosgrove - Fenny Stratford -
  Marsworth Jcn - Cowley Peachey Jcn - Bull's
  Bridge Jcn - Brentford

Allow 105 hours travelling the whole ring.
4 miles of tidal river, 98 miles of wide river, 46 miles
of narrow canal, 99 miles of wide canal, 2 tunnels, 1
aqueduct, 38 narrow locks, 137 wide locks.

The only major ring in the south of England has
everything - wide river and tidal waters, tunnels
and aqueducts, an original twisting narrow canal
following the contours of the land and a wide
canal improved as recently as 1937.

Visitor attractions
Kew Gardens
300 acres of botanical research, plant lables abound.
Restored Palm House (1840), the 'Princess of Wales
Conservatory' (1987), the 'Orangery' and Royal
Palace (1631) are part of the formal gardens but the
wider park has lake, arboretum and pagoda.
Tie up on the canal in Brentford. Cross Kew Bridge.
Richmond Park (1637)
2300 acre Royal Deer Park with many walks,
rhodedendron glades and the Royal Ballet School.
Tie up upstream of Richmond Bridge and climb up
steep Star and Garter Hill.
Ham House (1610)
Restored gardens (1975) to early design (1670) and
reinstated interior and tapestries of pre-Cromwellian
riverside mansion.

Oracle Shopping Centre, Kennet and Avon Canal, Reading

Tie up near Richmond Bridge. Use the Thames Path.
Twickenham Museum of Rugby
(Tel: 020 8892 8877)
Within the famous stadium developed on 'Billy
Williams' Cabbage Patch'.
Tie up near Eel Pie Island. Walk across High Street.
Hampton Court Palace
State Apartments of Henry VIII, King William III and
the Queen, Tudor kitchens, Georgian rooms, Wolsey
rooms and 60 acre palace garden with maze.
Tie up outside the Tijou Screen at the Privy Garden.
Desborough Island and Shepperton
Created by constuction of Desborough Cut (1935)
which is a short cut bypassing two attractive loops of
the river. Visit Shepperton Church Square.
Tie up alongside Shepperton riverside park.
Thorpe Park (Tel: 01932 562633)
Huge theme park in former gravel workings with
constantly increasing number of rides and exhibits.
Flume ride, boating lake, water-ski show and more.
Use Penton Hook Marina facilities. Cross A320. Or
tie up opposite Laleham Abbey near Harris
Boatbuilders. Use footpath away from river.
Runnymede (National Trust)
Magna Carta (1215) was the first formal document
limiting the powers of the Monarchy. Included the
right of navigation on the 'King's rivers'. Memorials
to J F Kennedy and the Commonwealth Air Forces.
Tie up alongside the riverbank meadows. Great.
Queen Mary's Dolls House, Windsor Castle
One of many attractions in the Castle, including state
apartments, gallery, St George's Chapel and Albert
Memorial Chapel. Walk around Home Park and the
riverfront. Cross Telford's Iron Bridge to Eton.
Historic buildings everywhere.
Tie up early on either bank. Busy in summer.
Legoland (Tel: 0990 626375)
Children reign supreme, 40 rides, bags of toy bricks
and the example of Miniland - miniature Brussels,
Amsterdam, Paris and London built with 20 million
toy bricks. Adventure playground and wood.
Tie up in Windsor. Short taxi ride.
Stanley Spencer Gallery
The 'Village from Heaven' inspired Spencer's work.
Christ Preaching at Cookham Regatta and Judgement
Day portray recognisable local landscape and local
people. Daily in summer, weekends only in winter.
Tie up near Cookham Bridge. Walk up to road
junction.
River and Rowing Museum
Olympic oarsman Sir Steve Redgrave's boat is the
most modern of exhibits showing the story of human
power through water. Thames history from source to
sea. Town Gallery has a spectacular audio visual
display. (Tel: 01491 415600)
Tie up on Mill Meadows, Henley.
Sonning Mill
18th century timber clad flour mill astride one of
three channels under Sonning Bridge. Now a small
theatre. Cocktail bar with restored mill wheel (1998).
Tie up downsream of Sonning Lock.
Blake's Lock Museum
Bakery, gentlemen's hairdresser, printer's workshop
from the 19th Century are reconstructed as part of a
museum celebrating Reading's Victorian industries.
Waterways displays. Restored gypsy ledge caravan.
Go into Kennet Mouth. Tie up beyond Blake's Lock.
Mapledurham House and Mill
Stunning river reach surrounded by beechwoods.

Marlow Weir

Working flour mill with wooden waterwheel and
shaft (restored 1977). Manor house (1588) was
fortified during Civil War (1643), family chapel.
Almshouses and church. Open weekend afternoons.
Tie up at Mapledurham Lock.
Beale Park
Kids' day out. Endangered species of cattle and
sheep, glorious wildfowl exhibits, narrow gauge
railway ride and finest owl enclosure in Europe - 16
species. In a pre-emptive strike against building on
the meadows, Gilbert Child-Beale made a wildlife
park.
Tie up at park's landing stage and river entrance.
Little Wittenham Footbridge
Venue for annual 'Pooh sticks' World championships.
Tie up at Day's Lock. Walk up to Wittenham Clumps.
Pendon Museum (Tel: 01865 407365)
Miniature railway runs through a lovingly created
1930s model landscape of the Vale of White Horse.
Constantly being extended. Excellent.
Tie up in Long Wittenham backwater. Open summer
weekend afternoons.
Godstow Abbey Ruins (1138-1646)
Nunnery, formerly site of pilgrimage to tomb of
Henry II's mistress Rosamond the Fair, poisoned by
Queen Eleanor (1177). The river crossing, domestic
buildings and hospice survived Cromwell's Fairfax
attacks. Hospice is now the 'Trout Inn'.
Tie up near Godstow Bridge.
Port Meadow
Freemen of Oxford were given the grazing rights for
cattle and horses by King Alfred when he founded
the City. They are jealously guarded and still
exercised to this day. Contains Bronze Age burials,
Port Meadow special geese (hybrid of wild and
domestic varieties) and on the lowest lying - and
never ploughed - area near Medley, a Site of Special
Scientific Interest (SSSI), with sweet floating grass
and water mint.
To explore on foot, tie up near Bossoms Boatyard. Go
east across Medley Footbridge to the Meadow.
Blenheim Palace
World Heritage Site. Vanburgh's house, Capability
Brown's parkland with lake, maze, herb garden.
Churchill's grave in nearby Blaydon churchyard.
Tie up near Bridge 216. 3 mile walk / taxi back?

Kirtlington Quarry
Picnic site directly accessible from the canal. Birdlife, footbridges and woodland.
Tie up near the warden's boat.

Rousham House
Uncommercialised 17th Century house with 150 portraits, William Kent landscape, cascades, statues, pigeon house, parterre. Garden open daily (Tel: 01869 347110).
Tie up at Bridge 206. Summer Wednesdays and Sundays.

Cropredy Bridge
Civil War battle (1644). Hordes also, come on 2nd weekend of every August to the Fairport Convention. End of Tom Rolt's first day on 'Cressy'.
Tie up north of Bridge 153.

Bygones Museum
Modest farm-based museum. Started as collection of everyday things from WWII but now gloriously expanded. Includes a complete chemist's shop and boatyard workshop, steam rollers and other vehicles.
Tie up near Bridge 144. Walk up to Claydon.

Althorp House and Garden
Spencer family home occupied continuously since 1586, 16 rooms to view. Round Oval Lake (1865) has island which is resting place of Diana, Princess of Wales. Exhibition celebrates her life and work. Open July and August. Book ahead (Tel: 0870 167 9000).
Tie up at Lock 13. 1 hour walk along country roads.

Woburn Abbey and Park (Tel: 01525 290666)
Safari Park, 3000 acre deer park, potter, sculpture gallery, antiques centre, in the grounds of a Cistercian Abbey (1145) which was surrendered when the Abbot was found guilty of treason (1538). Later given to Dukes of Bedford who, amongst other things, were instrumental in draining the Fens.
Tie up near Bridge 96. Take 5 mile taxi ride.

Bletchley Park
WWII Station X, forerunner of all intelligence gathering networks. Early computing assisted in code breaking. Museum run by volunteers.
Tie up near Bridge 96. Half hour walk / taxi back?

Waterway distractions

Richmond Half Tide Lock
A glorious Victorian structure (1894) formed of two pedestrian bridges with a huge set of gates swung between them. Lowered at every half tide they hold the river upstream at a steady level. Lock alongside available for navigation - at a price.
Tie up upstream, alongside Ranelagh Road.

Teddington Tidal Locks
Three separate locks operate only when the tide is right. Old boat rollers border the skiff lock, launch lock and huge barge lock which can take a tug and six barges. Pontoons of the Mulberry Harbour were sized to fit through the barge lock (1944).
Tie up upstream of the locks.

Thames Lock Keepers
At every one of 43 locks on the non-tidal Thames. Helpful, good humoured controllers of boats of every kind. Packing them in - steel first, GRP afterwards. In slack periods will ring ahead to warn the next lock you are coming. They could have it ready for you.
Greet them at Teddington Tidal Lock.

Jubilee River (1989-2001)
Seven miles of new channel, set up as flood relief for the River Thames around Maidenhead and Windsor. Navigable for light craft. Huge new wildlife habitat.
Tie up below Boulter's Lock.

Whitchurch Toll Bridge
Taking over the ferry rights (1792) the Company of Proprietors are still responsible for toll collection and bridge repair, three bridges and 300 years later.
Tie up at NT Pangbourne Meadows.

Goring Gap
Steep wooded chalk slopes define a narrow valley as the river breaks through the Chiltern Hills. Prehistoric ford replaced by a narrow bridge whose design reflects an earlier structure of wood. Intersection of Ridgeway with Thames Path.
Tie up south of lock. Walk around.

Wallingford Old Bridge
Seventeen medieval, ribbed stone arches span the floodplain to the east of castle earthworks of this ancient town (1130 charter). Only five span water. Dry moats and huge earthworks remain from Norman times. Saxon burh supported town walls. Excellent tiny museum (Tel: 01491 835065).
Tie up at moorings upstream of bridge. Walk around.

Swift Ditch, Abingdon
A cut (1635) widening the navigation through one of the three earliest locks on the river, bypassed 1790.
Tie up upstream of the modern Abingdon Lock. Walk.

Duke's Cut Lock (1789)
Built before levels on upper River Thames were controlled by weirs and locks, this lock had to cope with a wide variation of water levels. Sometimes the canal was higher than the river, at other times the river was in flood and higher than the canal. Thus gates on the original lock had to 'face both ways'. The recesses for the third set of gates can still be seen.
Tie up short of the junction. Look carefully.

Thrupp
Stone canalside village. Gunpowder Wharf next to old turnpike. Local club manages visitor moorings.
Tie up on allocated mooring.

Aynho Weir
Long weir with towpath over. Allows swollen river to cross the canal on the level.
Tie up beween Locks 32 and 33.

Tooley's Boatyard
Very early boatyard, established when Oxford Canal paused at Banbury for 12 years (1778). Now 'renovated' as part of Banbury Museum. Tooley family followed Tom Rolt's designs for refit of 'Cressy' as matrimonial home for his new wife. Start of voyage celebrated in his book 'Narrow Boat' - the catalyst which led to the formation of an early environmentally friendly campaigning charity - The

Inland Waterways Association.
Tie up alongside Castle Quay, Banbury.

Fenny Compton Tunnel (Cutting)
Narrow canal in cutting with very steep sides. Result of opening up two tunnels (1870).
Part of the summit pound.

Wormleighton
Small village church acts as landmark whilst the deep summit pound of Brindley's canal twists and turns its way along a single contour, giving sightings of the church spire on every quarter. Most confusing.
Oxford Canal's summit pound.

Braunston
Hub of the canal system, where early broad boats off-loaded onto narrowboat pairs to journey north. A Pickfords wharf, two boatyards, retired boatmen. Old canal course now a large marina. Tunnel nearby.
Tie up at Braunston Turn.

Blisworth Tunnel (1805)
One of the 'top three' tunnels (9170 feet). After a false start and flooding, a second surveyed line was completed replacing the double track horse tramway built across the top five years before.
Tie up at tunnel portal. Walk across the top?

Canal Museum, Stoke Bruerne
Original waterways museum, based on a private collection. Canal clothing, brasses, signs, models, paintings, photographs plus larger exhibits of butty boat cabin, steam engines, boat weighing scales.
Tie up south of tunnel mouth.

Great Ouse Aqueduct (35 feet high)
Cast Iron aqueduct on stone pillars (1811) replaced one in brick which had collapsed after only 3 years (1805-8). Prior to that temporary locks had allowed trade to flow. Evidence on the valley floor.
Tie up north of Cosgrove Lock. See start of Old Stratford and Buckingham Arm.

Marsworth Reservoirs
Main water supply for Tring summit. Four huge reservoirs. Tringford Pumping Station supplying the Wendover Arm. Now acknowledged as wildlife haven.
Tie up at summit or by Bridge 132. Walk around six

Typical Grand Union Canal wide lock, Stoke Bruerne

Re-instated lift bridge, Factory Street, Banbury

miles of waymarked paths.

Cassiobury Park
Surveyed line of the canal went through Earl of Essex's private park, so he insisted on highly ornamental stone bridge for his main driveway. Now a public park - the bridge survives.
Tie up near Bridge 164.

Batchworth Lock
Hub of many watery walks. Short arm to old wharf, recreational 'Aquadrome', restoration of working boat 'Roger', Canal Visitor Centre (Tel: 01923 788382).
Tie up below lock.

Three Bridges
Unique intersection - road over canal over rail.
Tie up at top of Hanwell Flight.

Worth a detour

Little Venice
Lock free Paddington Arm. Visit London.
13 miles each way. Allow 7 hours.

Abbey Moorings, Reading
Pass through Blake's Lock and turn right into the backwater. Tie up and walk through town to the canalside Oracle Shopping Centre.
¼ mile, 1 lock each way. Allow 1 hour.

Suggested Guide Books
David Sharp *The Thames Path* Aurum Press,1996
Anthony Burton *The Grand Union Canal Walk* Aurum Press,1993

i Tourist Information
Richmond: Tel: 020 8940 9125
Kingston upon Thames Tel: 020 8547 5592
Windsor Tel: 01753 852010
Maidenhead Tel: 01628 781110
Marlow Tel: 01628 483597
Henley-on-Thames Tel: 01491 578034

Reading Tel: 0118 956 6226
Wallingford Tel: 01491 826972
Abingdon Tel: 01235 522711
Oxford Tel: 01865 726871
Banbury Tel: 01295 259855
Northampton Tel: 01604 604180
Milton Keynes Tel: 01908 232525
Hemel Hempstead Tel: 01442 234222
Uxbridge Tel: 01895 250600

GEO *Cruising Maps*
GEOprojects: *Thames, the river and the path*
GEOprojects: *Oxford Canal*
GEOprojects: *Grand Union Canal map 2, Braunston to Kings Langley*
GEOprojects: *Grand Union Canal map 3, Fenny Stratford to the Thames*

Start Points

2	Adelaide Marine Ltd	**50**	Canalboat Holidays Ltd
2	London & Home Counties Narrowboat Holidays	**58**	College Cruisers
		68	Ferryline Cruisers
6	Alvechurch Boat Centres	**81**	Kennet Cruises
15	Anglo Welsh Waterway Holidays	**82**	Kingcraft
15	Oxfordshire Narrowboats	**83**	Kris Cruisers
26	Avalon Narrowboat Co	**88**	Napton Narrowboats
30	Berry Brook Boats	**90**	Nationwide Narrowboats
30	London & Home Counties Narrowboat Holidays	**95**	Reading Marine Company
37	Blisworth Tunnel Boats Ltd	**97**	Red Line Cruisers
39	Bridge Boats Ltd	**117**	Union Canal Carriers Ltd
39	Caversham Boat Services	**125**	Weltonfield Narrowboats Ltd
41	Bridgewater Boats	**129**	Wyvern Shipping Co Ltd
47	Calcutt Boats Ltd	**130**	Chertsey Meads Marine
		131	Swancraft Boat Services Ltd

The Fens

Flat lands, birds and soaring skies.

Grand Union Canal (1805)
Fenny Stratford - Cosgrove - Blisworth - Gayton - Rothersthorpe Flight - Northampton
River Nene Navigation (1490, 1730, 1761, 1935)
Northampton - Wellingborough - Oundle - Fotheringhay - Peterborough
Middle Level Navigations (1631-51, 1810-44, 1874)
Peterborough - Stanground - Kings - Whittlesley - Old River - Upwell - Well Creek - Salter's Lode
Great Ouse Navigation (1904, 1978)
Salter's Lode - Denver Sluice - Ely - Pope's Corner - Earith - Huntingdon - St Neots - Bedford

Allow 70 hours from Milton Keynes to Bedford
5 miles of narrow canal, 24 miles of wide canal, 30 miles of navigable drain, 130 miles of wide river, 1 tunnel, 2 aqueducts, 17 narrow locks, 72 wide locks.

Down a lock flight into two classic meandering English rivers and the mysteries of shrinking former marshlands. The joy of this adventure is the isolation but the need is for a little foresight. Pack lots of victuals, use facilities when you can.

Visitor attractions

Ferry Meadows, Peterborough (500 acres)
Nene Valley Steam Railway follows the river and passes through 2500 acres of woodland, lakes and backwaters. Popular since Victorian times.
Tie up short of the golf course.

The Embankment, Peterborough
Tree lined, on a wide sweep of river, close to the compact city centre and its Cathedral Square,
Tie up next to boaters facilities and the Key Theatre.

Flag Fen Excavations (Tel: 01733 313414)
Ongoing archaeological dig exposing Bronze Age Fen habitation - 3000 year-old timbers, pigs, sheep.
Tie up at the Embankment.
Walk across city centre.

Welney Wildfowl and Wetlands Centre
Internationally recognised, visited every year by thousands of migratory birds. Boardwalk, pond dipping. Hides and accommodation.
(Tel: 01353 860711)
Tie up at Welney on New Bedford 'River'.

Oliver Cromwell's House
The Cromwells were a landed family hereabouts and Oliver lived here for ten years. Restored to reflect his period, it houses the Tourist Information Centre.
Tie up by Ely Maltings.

Wicken Sedge Fen
Oldest nature reserve in the country (1899). (Tel: 01535 720274)
Stop at Wicken Lode. Usable by short craft under 22 feet.

Stretham Old Engine
Hero of a breach (1919), this steam engine lifted 120 tons an hour for 47 days until repair was made. Now electricity has allowed retirement.
Tie up upstream of the bridge.

Earith
Fortified earthworks from the Civil War guard the junctions of the Ouse with the Bedford 'rivers'. Short reach affected by tides.
Tie up alongside one of two pubs or in the marina.

Godmanchester Bridges
A Roman fort overlooked the bridge for the roads to London, York and Cambridge. A Chinese 'willow pattern' bridge leads across onto an island and backwaters past Georgian house gardens down to the water.
Tie up on the Old Lock wall. Follow the Ouse Valley Way into town.

Bunyan Museum, Huntingdon
Grandson of a waterman, John Bunyan, preacher (1628) spent 12 years in gaol for refusing to be silent and later started 'Pilgrims Progress' during a further detention. Museum celebrates his fame.
Tie up at Mill Meadow. Explore this County Town.

Earith. One of the largest structures on the waterways, it succumbed to forces of angry 'Fens Tigers' (1653) and to forces of nature (1713). Finally renewed by Rennie (1749), although reinforced since. If the tide is out you go downhill with the river, but high tide means you have to lock up to sea level.

St Ives Bridge (pedestrians only)
Six-arched stone bridge (1425) replaced the monks' wood structure (1107). Wooden drawbridge inserted at the southern end during the Civil War (1645) is now replaced with a different design of arch.
St Leger's Chapel (1426, 1930) on the central span is one of only three bridge chapels in the country. Also used as toll house, inn and residence. Now open.
Tie up upstream of bridge.

Bedford: Upper and Lower Rivers
Through the heart of Bedford, the river runs past itself on two levels with a single lock and tumbling weirs between. Rowing clubs enjoy the calm of the wide straight upper river with its many footbridges and well kept 'Embankment'.
Tie up on Mill Meadow. Good also, for a visit by car.

Worth a detour

Jesus Lock, Cambridge (1837)
Past Wicken Fen and a walk to the Backs.
14½ miles, 3 locks each way. Allow 6 hours.
High Lode, Ramsey
Meres and Fens galore, turning for max 25 foot boats.
Access - from Floods Ferry on the Old River Nene
8 miles, 0 locks each way. Allow 4 hours.
Port of Wisbech
Long adventure through Dog in a Doublet Lock onto the tidal Nene and to the high banks and varying water levels of the Town Quay.
19 miles, 1 tidal lock each way. Allow 10 hours.

Future possibilities

Years ago (1810, 1892) a waterway link from the Grand Union Canal to Bedford was proposed. A scheme to make the link before 2010 is under consultation and would open up at least three major possibilities:-

For narrowboats using Rothersthorpe Lock flight - a major 'more time' ring of 78 hours travelling time.

For broader beam boats from both the Fens and the Grand Union Canal - the chance to cruise each others' waters.

For broader beam boats whose owners wish to travel from Bristol or Oxford to Cambridge.

📖 *Suggested Guide Book*
Derek Bowskill *The Norfolk Broads and Fens*
Opus, 1999

ℹ️ *Tourist Information*
Wisbech Tel: 01945 583263
Ely Tel: 01353 662062
Cambridge Tel: 01366 387440
Peterborough Tel: 01773 452336
Huntingdon Tel: 01480 388588
Northampton Tel: 01604 622677
Bedford Tel: 01234 215226

Start Points

6 Alvechurch Boat Centres		**70** Fox Boats
37 Blisworth Tunnel Boats Ltd		**89** Nationwide Narrowboats
40 Bridge Boatyard		**90** Nationwide Narrowboats

Waterway distractions

Rothersthorpe Flight of Narrow Locks
Thirteen locks in quick order plus four descend a hill overlooking Northampton and the Nene Valley.
Licence for river required. See Gayton boatyards.
Middle Level Navigations (Tel: 01733 566413)
To keep huge former marshlands dry, excess water is pumped from fields at lower levels up into channels at higher levels which then drain to the sea. Earlier wind pumps gave way to steam, diesel then electicity. There are three major levels. One, by the Dutchman Vermuyden, made for the Earl of Bedford (now shrunk below sea level), this Middle Level and the

final level of rivers held from flooding by high banks.
Drop from rivers at Stanground & Salter's Lode Locks.
Dog in a Doublet (Tel: 01733 202219).
Restaurant with accompanying tidal lock (1937).
Check with lock keeper before approaching.
Well Creek (8 miles)
Part of the Nene-Ouse navigation link. Saved from abandonment by the Well Creek Trust (1975), as their vital contribution to connect the waterway network.
Denver Tidal Sluice (VHF 16/17, Tel: 01366 382340)
A structure to protect the meandering Great Ouse River from the extra waters of the incoming tides which are sent instead up the Hundred Foot Drain to

Two Roses Ring

Engineering and countryside on the grandest scale.

Bridgewater Canal (1769, 1799)
Castlefield - Waters Meeting - Worsley - Leigh

Leeds and Liverpool Canal (1816, 1820)
Leigh - Wigan - Blackburn - Burnley - Skipton - Bingley - Saltaire - Granary Wharf, Leeds

Aire and Calder Navigation (1702)
Granary Wharf, Leeds - Castleford Jcn - Fall Ing Lock

Calder and Hebble Navigation (1770)
Fall Ing Lock. - Cooper Bridge Jcn - Salterhebble Locks - Sowerby Bridge

Rochdale Canal (1804)
Sowerby Bridge - Tuel Lane Lock - Fallingroyd Tunnel - Longlees Lock 36 - Hollingworth Lake - Rochdale - Ducie Street Jcn - Castlefield

Allow 94 hours travelling, which would take 16 days at a slog of 6 hours every day.
178 miles of wide canal, 18 miles of canalised rivers, 4 tunnels, 214 wide locks including the deepest in the country (Tuel Lane Lock) and 39 swing bridges.
Seven Wonders:
Barton Swing Aqueduct
Burnley Embankment
Bingley Five Rise Locks

50

Serving both Lancashire and Yorkshire, this is one of the few rings that is available for wide beam boats. It is a major ring, large in every sense of the word. The Rochdale Canal constructed the highest concentration of wide locks in the country (92 locks), the Leeds and Liverpool Canal is the longest single canal (127 miles) and the Yorkshire rivers flow strongly down their steep valleys. The whole lot was designed to shift huge amounts of heavy cargo, up to 70 tons at a time. First the Duke of Bridgewater's coal to Manchester and then all goods carried by the barges of the Yorkshire rivers.

It makes for a seriously enjoyable, but long, trip up into the moors of Pendle, the Dales of Yorkshire and across the high Pennine Ridge, using waterways that are delightfully uncrowded plus the challenges of operating the huge gates of wide locks - some in staircase formation.

Visitor attractions

Granada Studios
Coronation Street and all that jazz.
Tie up in Castlefield Basin.

Museum of Science and Industry
(Tel: 0161 832 2244)
Celebration of the saying 'what Manchester does today, the world does tomorrow'. Air and Space, industrial power - waterwheels to turbines, story of electricity, textiles, printing and machine tools. The first passenger railway station.
Tie up in Castlefield Basin

The Lowry
Three art galleries and two theatres on a headland at Salford Quays.
Use the new Pomona Lock and turn left.

Astley Green Colliery Museum
Only headgear and engine house left in Lancashire. 3300 horse power twin tandem compound steam winding engine. Underground railway locomotive collection. Wharf for coal to Barton Power Station.
Open Tuesday, Thursday and Sunday afternoons.

Wigan Pier
Small coal staithe at the centre of a series of three themed attractions linked by a waterbus. The 2500 horse power Trencherfield Engine is demonstrated every half hour running a 27 ton flywheel. Wigan Pier Theatre Company plays in 'The Way We Were' exhibits.
Tie up near Wigan Bottom Lock 87.

Haigh Hall
Children's amusements, miniature railway, crazy golf, glasshouses and waymarked nature trails in huge parkland run by Wigan Corporation. Hall itself based in pre-Tudor mansion, rebuilt 1840.
Tie up at Bridge 60.

Withnall Fold
Terraced cottages around a formal square were home to workers in the paper mill. Filter beds along the river are now centrepiece for a nature reserve.
Tie up near Bridge 88.

Pendle Witches: Demdike, Device and Chattox
Executed (1612) Lancaster, two rival family heads lived on the moors and terrorised the people. Full story in Pendle Heritage Centre.
Tie up near Barrowford Locks.

Pennine Way, Gargrave
Long distance footpath crosses the canal and soon enters Yorkshire Dales National Park. Go for a short or long walk about. Stripling River Aire in village - worth a stroll.
Tie up by Lock 32. Cycle hire Tel: 01756 748030

Skipton Castle
Best preserved, most complete 12th Century Medieval castle overlooking Lord Thanet's Canal. After Civil War siege (1645) roof was only allowed to be rebuilt if it was too weak to support a cannon. Dungeon.
Tie up in Skipton.

Embsay Steam Railway (1888)
Steam railway every Sunday plus other times.
Tie up in Skipton. (Tel: 01756 795189)

Settle-Carlisle Railway (from Skipton Station)
Subject of campaign to stop closure. A ride takes you through far flung valleys and across the (then-deteriorating) magnificent viaduct at Ribblehead.
Tie up near Bridge 176, let the train take the strain.

Bolton Abbey
Historic estate on River Wharf. Medieval buildings. Priory ruins. 75 miles of footpaths.
Tie up in Skipton. Grab a taxi.

Trencherfield Engine, Lock 87, Wigan

Bronte Parsonage Museum, Haworth
Charlotte, Emily and Anne survived their mother's early death to grow up with their Reverend father and become well known authors. (Tel: 01535 647131)
Tie up near Bridge 197. Use Keighley and Worth Valley Railway or 5 mile taxi ride up Worth Valley.

Saltaire
Applicant for World Heritage status, stone built town (1850) with everything Sir Titus Salt could think of for his employees except pubs. Salt's mill now hosts David Hockney's work - son of the area.
Tie up near Bridge 207A.

Leeds Industrial Museum
(Tel: 0113 263 7861)
Housed at Armley Mills. Everything to do with industrial Leeds, working machinery of all kinds, plus a cinema of the 1920s.
Tie up near Bridge 225A.

Royal Armouries Museum
Home of national collection of arms and armour, including the biggest suit of all - for an elephant. Jousting and falconry in the Tiltyard.
Turn into Clarence Dock and tie up.

Thwaite Mills
Two waterwheels collapsed (1975) and closed the business, but the mill building (1872) now gives a taste of working conditions in a stone-grinding mill.
Tie up canalside below Knostrop Fall Lock.

St Aidan's Opencast Mine
Coalmine with new channel built alongside after a major breach flooded everything nearby (1988).
To the north of the navigation at Allerton Bywater.

Piece Hall, Halifax
'Exchange and Mart' for the cloth woven by cottage workers in the hills around. Superb architecture.
Tie up near Salterhebble Locks. Walk up the hill.

Eureka! (Tel: 01426 983191)
Over 400 hands-on exhibits for anyone to touch, listen and smell. Food, television, toilets, all manner of subjects, designed for kids of all ages.
Tie up near Salterhebble Locks. Walk up the hill.

Merchant's Bridge, Castlefield, Manchester

Walkley's Clogs
Only surviving clog mill. Exhibits on clog making, coin counterfeiting and much more.
Tie up above Lock 7.

Hollingworth Lake Country Park
Victorian tourist resort developed around feeder reservoir. Use visitor centre and waymarked walks.
Tie up at Heald Lane Bridge.

East Lancs Steam Railway (Tel: 0161 764 7790)
Runs between Heywood, Bury and Rawtenstall.
Tie up at Castleton Station. Catch the train.

Waterway distractions

Castlefield
Terminus of Duke of Bridgewater's private canal. Specialized wharfage and warehouses were used to off-load potatoes, groceries, general merchandise, timber and slate and there was, of course, a coal yard.
Take your boat to the far end of the complex where Knott Mill Packet Station was the boarding point for high speed lock free journeys to Worsley, Wigan and Runcorn, with onward boats to Liverpool.

Barton Swing Aqueduct (1893)
Replaced Brindley's original stone arches (1761) when the Manchester Ship Canal cut the line of the older canal. 1450 tonnes of water filled cassion is sealed and turns to let the big ships past.
Tie up. Walk down to the park by the Ship Canal.

Worsley Delph
Underground mines driven horizontally for a total of 55 miles were drained by navigable channels on two levels connected by a short underground inclined plane. The system ran out to the surface at Worsley. Coal was then delivered by water to Manchester.
Stop at Worsley Green. See amenity society boards.

Wigan Flight
Major flight of 21 locks lifting the Leeds and Liverpool Canal to meet the southern pound of the Lancaster Canal.
Follow the lock keeper's directions.

Burnley Embankment
3500 feet long, 60 feet high a 'straight mile' looks over the terracotta chimneys of hundreds of terraced houses. Major engineering achievement and wonder of the waterways.
Tie up part way along for access to the town.

Foulridge Lower Reservoir
Sits over the line of the Foulridge Tunnel. One of five needed to make good the water flow away from the summit.
Tie up at the tunnel entrance. Footpath over the top.

Foulridge Tunnel (4900 feet)
Famous for the exploit of a cow which fell in, faced the wrong way and swam the length of the tunnel. Revived by the administration of brandy.
Tie up and take your turn through.

Greenberfield Locks
First set of locks curving down from the summit, replacing a staircase. Set in glorious countryside.
Locks 42-44.

Lord Thanet's Canal
Built as a private canal to meet a track from M'lord's quarries. If you want to turn at the end, your boat must be less than 35 feet. Also known as Springs Branch.
Tie up in Skipton. Walk up the towpath - well worth it.

Bingley Five Rise Locks (1774)
True wonder, standing in the countryside, dropping 60 feet under lock keeper supervision. No power tools to build it, a massive achievement. Repeated four times on a lesser scale nearby.
Tie up, walk down and observe before your descent.

Stanley Ferry Aqueducts
Forerunner (1839) of Sydney Harbour Bridge, elegant twin arches hold up the trough. Parallel concrete aqueduct (1981) not so elegant.
Tie up near Stanley Ferry Marina.

Fall Ing Lock, Wakefield
Start of Calder and Hebble cut, running above the meandering river and entering handspike country.
Tie up at Figure of Three Locks, Work out the system.

Tuel Lane Lock (19'6")
Coupled with a 'tunnel', 50 yards of works were the first stage connection of the Rochdale Canal to the system.
Tie up and ask the lock keeper Tel: 0860 336750.

Fallingroyd Tunnel
No towpath, but the trip boat is horse-drawn - so look out for the slow 'legging' process inside the tunnel.
When entering the tunnel, be aware, take care.

Great Wall, Todmorden (1858)
Railway sidings squeezed into the valley supported by this sheer wall of tens of thousands of bricks.
Tie up at Lock 19.

Longlees Lock 36
One end of the summit pound at 600 feet above sea level, restored (1979) by the Rochdale Canal Society in the days when such efforts were a supreme act of faith. Give thanks and £6 for a Summit Brass Plaque.
Summit pound is wide and deep, passing through the greatest scenery. Turnpike nearby, rail tunnel below.

Rochdale Nine: Locks 84-92
When all the rest of the Rochdale Canal was closed by its private owners, these locks were open (at a price), but on condition the Ashton Canal remained navigable. This was achieved for many years and now the whole Rochdale Canal is no longer privately owned.
Proceed carefully through the urban 'tunnels'.

Worth a detour

Bridgewater Canal to Runcorn
A lock free run in Cheshire. Waters Meeting, Bollin Embankment, Lymm, Preston Brook Junction.
29½ miles, 0 locks each way. Allow 11 hours.

Ribble Link to Preston
A tidal crossing and a taste of the Lancaster Canal. Wigan Pier, Burscough Junction, Rufford Branch, Tarleton Tidal Lock, Ribble Link and Ashton Basin.
30 miles, 23 locks each way. Allow 26 hours.

Sir John Ramsden's Canal
Also known as the Huddersfield Broad Canal. A short trip from Cooper Bridge Junction to Huddersfield town centre and Aspley Basin.
3½ mile, 9 locks each way. Allow 4 hours.

📖 ***Suggested Guide Book***
John Lower *The South Pennine Ring* Hallamshire, 1998

ℹ️ ***Tourist Information***
Manchester Tel: 0161 643 0988
Wigan Tel: 01942 825677
Blackburn Tel: 01254 532277
Burnley Tel: 01282 455485
Skipton Tel: 01756 792809
Bradford Tel: 01274 753678
Leeds Tel: 0113 242 5242
Wakefield Tel: 01282 666704
Huddersfield Tel: 01484 223200
Halifax Tel: 01422 368725
Hebden Bridge Tel: 01422 843831
Todmorden Tel: 01706 818181
Rochdale Tel: 01706 356592

🗺️ ***Cruising Maps***
GEOprojects: *Leeds and Liverpool Canal*
GEOprojects: *Huddersfield Broad and Narrow Canals with the Ashton Canal*
GEOprojects: *South Pennine Ring* (2002)

Start Points

16 Anglo Welsh Waterway Holidays	**59** Constellation Cruises Ltd
22 Arlen Hire Boats	**84** Lower Park Marina
24 Aspley Wharf Marina	**94** Pennine Cruisers
32 Black Prince Holidays	**104** Shepley Bridge Marina Ltd
34 Black Prince Holidays	**106** Shire Cruisers
34 Silsden Boats	**108** Snaygill Boats Ltd
55 Claymoore Navigation Ltd	

Wide beamed trip boat, Hebden Bridge

Royal Armouries Museum, Clarence Dock, Leeds

The Broads

When many people think 'boating' they think 'Broads'. Popular for almost one hundred years, hirebases offer a wide range of different style boats, from the original 'swept out wherries' through wide motor cruisers between 25 and 45 foot long sleeping from 2 to 12, to a yacht fleet which sleeps 2 to 6 people. With lots of space on the water (9000 acres), the five rivers are wide enough and the lakes broad enough to allow an excellent variety of conditions for regattas and recreational sailing.

Carved out of an area of flat fens, the broads themselves are the flooded remains of peat extraction activity during 350 years (12th-14th centuries). At that time Norwich was the prosperous centre of one of the most densely populated areas in England and had run out of forests to fuel its needs. Peat fires became the norm and thousands of marshmen toiled daily digging at the pits - which sometimes flooded before they had finished and thus commenced the long slow regeneration process of silting, reedbeds, fen and carr.

Under the stewardship of the Broads Authority (1988) increasing recognition has been given to the unique ecological status of the area. It is an internationally renowned wetland containing many designated Sites of Special Scientific Interest and actions have been in place to restore some broads to a cleaner, healthier and more diverse water environment.

As a result, watching nature from nonpowered craft, electrically driven day boats or your own hired boat is especially rewarding at certain times and certain areas. Check with the people at your hire base. Most times heron, coot, mallard, moorhen, great crested grebe and swans are close to the water with sedge warbler, blackcap, bearded tit and kingfisher flitting by. Animals such as stoats, weasels, otters and water voles can often be seen. A veritable cornucopia.

Rivers and channels
River Ant
  Dilham Staithe - Ant Mouth
River Bure
  Coltishall Lock - Bure Mouth
River Thurne
  Catfield Common - Thurne Mouth
River Yare
  River Wensum, Norwich - Great Yarmouth
River Waveney
  Geldeston Lock - River Yare
Haddiscoe New Cut
  Reedham - St Olaves
Oulton Dyke
  Waveney - Oulton Broad

Allow 80 hours travelling to cover the whole area. 125 miles of river, 4 miles of wide canal, 1 lock at Mutford.

Virtually lock free with gentle tidal effects, but be aware of bridges that apparently sink after rain raises water levels in the rivers flowing beneath.

River Ant

Visitor attractions
Stalham
Georgian market town at end of Stalham Dyke.
Tie up at Stalham Staithe. Walk to Hickling Broad.
Sutton Windmill Broads Museum
Nine storey mill (1789-1940) stands on higher ground away from water. Views of sea coast and flatlands, Horsey Mere and Hickling Broad.
Tie up at Sutton Staithe. Short walk.
How Hill Nature Reserve (Broads Authority)
Electric boat takes a waterborne trail beside reed beds, marsh meadows with grazing cattle and carr woodland, all managed as it might have been a century ago. Toad Hole, a small marshman's cottage, tells the story. Walking nature trail, 350 acres.
Tie up at the dedicated moorings.
Neatishead
Lime Kiln Dyke remembers one of the diverse industries of the area. Narrow.
Tie up at Gay's staithe or the Neatishead Parish Staithe.

Waterway distractions
North Walsham and Dilham Canal (1826-1935) (limit of navigation)
At present Dilham Dyke to Honing Lock is navigable only by hand-powered craft, although in the days before roads were improved, six locks had allowed wherries to trade 8½ miles through marshland to North Welsham.
Powered craft may continue to Dilham Staithe.
Ant Mouth
Confluence of the River Ant and the River Bure.
Turn left towards Great Yarmouth.

River Bure

Visitor attractions
Bure Valley Railway (Tel: 01263 733858)
Ride on a 15 inch gauge railway nine miles to Aylsham, with the 'Huff 'n' Puff' cycle path along the whole distance.
Tie up upstream of Wroxham railway bridge. Maybe take the train one way and return on hired bikes.
Three Rivers Race, Horning
Two day event, part of Annual August Regatta. Horning's Lower Street serves a multitude of small private side dykes and one large entry to hirebases.
Tie up at Horning Parish Staithe or Horning Ferry.
Broadland Conservation Centre
Floating two storey, thatched building with displays downstairs and views from upstairs. Ranworth Broad was isolated from the river, suction dredged (1982), now undergoing bio-manipulation to produce clearer waters and improved wildlife habitat.
Tie up at Ranworth Staithe and use boardwalks, or use a temporary mooring near Ferry Point.
St Helen's Church, Ranworth
Cathedral of the Broads, views from the tower extend to North and South Broads. 97 steep steps. In the nave a painted rood screen and an illustrated hymn book in medieval Latin - Sarum Antiphoner. Tea gardens outside in a coach house.
Tie up at Ranworth Staithe. Follow road round right.
St Benet's Abbey (1020-1545)
From a commanding position on a 20 foot hump (known as a 'holm'), this Abbey saw many a trauma

Sunset at St Olaves

(Peasants Revolt 1381) but escaped the Dissolution. Abbot was then transferred to be Bishop of Norwich with a remit for the Abbey's upkeep. Sadly, within ten years it had died of neglect. Ruins are used for an annual service conducted by the Bishop.
Only accessible by water.

Stracey Arms Windpump (1833)
Restored and open in summer. Stopping point before the run to Great Yarmouth.
Tie up near the pub.

Waterway distractions

Coltishall Lock (limit of navigation)
Remaining lock of five provided (1779-1928) to give water access to Aylsham. Busy for over 100 years.
Turn before the cut. Tie up near the common.

Wroxham Bridge
Vulnerable narrow low headroom bridge at the start of the idea of Broads Cruising over 150 years ago. Over 15 hirebases. Busy on 'changeover days'.
Tie up upstream of the railway bridge.

Salhouse Broad
Gently navigable broad, opposite the non-navigable Hoveton Great Broad Nature Reserve.
Tie up at any of three moorings.

Cockshoot Broad (Norfolk Wildlife Trust)
White water lilies in spring, damsel flies in summer, coot, heron, tufted duck, crested grebe all year. The boardwalk leads to hides overlooking water, wet woodland and sedge, where willow tit, treecreeper, chiffchaff and wren may be heard if not seen.
Tie up opposite Ferry Inn. Cross the dyke and enter.

Bure Mouth and Breydon Water
Confluence with the River Yare is under two bridges, hire craft turn right to enter Breydon Water.
Be sure to follow marked channel.

River Thurne

Visitor attractions

Horsey Windpump (National Trust)
Restored (1948) photogenic windpump stands on its feeder channel to Horsey Mere (also NT).
Tie up before the staithe, you may need to back out.

Ludham
13th century St Catherine's church with catherine wheel symbols high in the roof timbers. Hunters Yard is home to the Norfolk Heritage Fleet. 60 year old mahogany sailing boats for hire.
Tie up at the Ludham Parish Staithe.

Waterway distractions

Hickling Broad (1926) (limit of navigation)
Apart from cuts to Waxham and the navigable feeder from Horsey Windpump, the largest of the broads (500 acres) is the shallow start of the River Thurne. Locals who windsurf and launch trailboats, maybe know the shallows better than most. Visitors should follow the marked channels. Reedbeds hide many timid species. Home to the large swallowtail butterfly. Replica shallow draughted 'Reed Lighter' gives 2 hour trips amongst the wildlife.
Tie up at Deep Dyke or Rush Hill. Listen.

Potter Heigham Medieval Bridge
Notoriously low headroom. Affected both by the difference between spring and neap tides and the amount of rain that has fallen upstream.
Ask for pilotage help, Tel: 01692 670460 (free to hirers).

Reedham on the River Yare

Thurne Dyke
Nearly two foot rise and fall of the tide makes this narrow dyke subject to curious currents.
Tie up at tiny Thurne village. Not too tight.

Thurne Mouth
Confluence of the River Thurne and the River Bure.
Continue straight towards Great Yarmouth.

River Waveney

Visitor attractions

Beccles
Saxon seaport, supplying herring. Now the closest village to the river, it has the church where Horatio Nelson's parents were married, an excellent museum and Roos Hall - a red brick manor house with ghosts.
Tie up between the bridges.

Beccles Marshes
One of ten soft areas that prevent road crossings between here and St Olaves, 14 miles away by water.
Take care at Beccles Bridge, only start when you know you can finish.

Waveney River Centre (Tel: 01502 677343)
Restaurant, pub, heated swimming pool on an extensive waterside boating and caravan centre.
Tie up on their free moorings.

Pleasurewood Hills (Tel: 01502 508200)
Theme park, thrill rides and miniature railway.
4 miles north of Lowestoft. Tie up on Oulton Broad, grab a taxi or catch a bus to Tesco's.

Lowestoft
Maritime Museum charting seafaring history. Royal Naval Patrol Museum, Marina Theatre, fish market and many seaside delights.
Tie up near Oulton Broad South Station. Go by train.

Somerleyton Hall (Rebuilt 1846)
Victorian garden, park and clock. Sir Morton Peto built Lowestoft Harbour, rebuilt Westminster Parliament and this Hall. The clock was originally ordered for Parliamentarians but cost too much for them.
Moor at Somerleyton Staithe. Walk beyond the village.

Herringfleet Mill
Catching the wind in woven sails, this is a unique survival of the early type of windpump (1750s).
No convenient moorings, can be seen from the river.

Burgh Castle: Roman Gariannonum
Roman shore fort, early monastery, Norman castle.
Tie up at the 48 hour moorings. Limit of Great Yarmouth Port Authority.

Waterway distractions
Geldeston Lock (limit of navigation)
Farthest downstream of the three locks that once gave access and prosperity to Bungay (1670-1929).
Now disused. Tie up and turn downstream.
Oulton Broad (130 Acres)
Crowded home of all the watersports you can imagine. The earliest power boat racing club in the country, windsurfing.
Many moorings. Walk to Boatworld - exhibition of boatbuilding skills. Beware powerboat racing on Thursday evenings and Bank Holidays.

Brundall
Grander settlement with large waterside homes and home to some of the most luxurious Broads craft.
Tie up across the road from the station for rail-borne side trips to Norwich or Great Yarmouth
Surlingham Marsh (RSPB)
Circular walk (1-2 miles) starts from the Church. Reed screens and hide allow quiet observation.
Tie up at Surlingham Ferry. Wellies essential.
Strumpshaw Fen Nature Reserve (RSPB)
Five miles of mown trails. Reedbeds, woodland and grazing marshes. Lots of birds.
Tie up opposite Buckenham Ferry.
Strumpshaw Hall Steam Museum
(Tel: 01603 714535)
Two fairground organs and traction engines galore. A compound beam engine from Croydon waterworks

Waterway distractions
Breydon Water: pivot of the Broads
Formerly the sea estuary for the Yare and Waveney Rivers, Breydon Water is joined by the River Bure at its outlet to the sea through Great Yarmouth. At low tide a vast expanse of soft mud is exposed except along the carefully buoyed channel.
Negotiating Breydon Water is easier if the ebb (7 hours) and flow (5 hours) of the tides is given due consideration. Find out their timings and enter at slack low water. At any state of the tide be sure to follow the carefully marked channel, otherwise you risk becoming a stick-in-the-mud and will be left high and dry.

📖 *Suggested Guide Book*
Derek Bowskill: *The Norfolk Broads and Fens* Opus, 1999

ℹ️ *Tourist Information*
Beccles Tel: 01502 713196
Great Yarmouth Tel: 01493 332095
Hoveton Tel: 01603 782281
How Hill Tel: 01692 678763
Potter Heigham Tel: 01692 670779
Ranworth Tel: 01603 270453
Great Yarmouth Tel: 01493 842195
Lowestoft Tel: 01502 523000
Norwich Tel: 01603 666071

🚲 *Broads Bike Hire*
Acle Bridge, Gay's Staithe, Hickling Staithe, Hoveton, Ludham Bridge, Reedham Quay, Sutton Staithe and Thurne Staithe (Tel: 01603 782281)

🗺️ *Cruising Maps*
GEOprojects: The Broads

Greylay geese, Salhouse Broad

Mutford Lock (Tel: 01502 531778)
Exit from Oulton Broad into Lake Lothing, through Lowestoft Inner Harbour, under Town Bridge, the Outer Harbour and into the turbulent North Sea.
Not available to hire craft, others might request a berth at the Royal Norfolk and Suffolk Yacht Club.
St Olaves Bridge
Windpump (1910) and Priory (1216) are downstream.
Tie up away from the eddies near the bridge.

River Yare

Visitor attractions
City of Norwich (Charter 1194) (limit of navigation)
Formerly a major port for trade with Europe. Watergate at Pulls Ferry defended the short canal dug to get Caen Stone up the final part of its journey from France to the Cathedral building site. Birthplace of Mr Thomas Bignold's Norwich Union (1792) and Mr Jeremiah Colman's excellent mustard (1804).
Moor at Norwich Yacht Station, the only legal place.
Bramerton Woods End
An opportunity to sample a gentler village ambiance.
Tie up at the Parish Staithe.

has a huge diameter (18 foot) flywheel (1893).
Tie up opposite Buckenham Ferry.
Hardley Cross
Monument to arguements. On the boundary of jurisdiction between Norwich and Great Yarmouth, it was the annual meeting place to settle disputes.
At the confluence of the Chet and Yare Rivers.
Reedham
Sitting between two moveable river crossings. Upstream a chain ferry takes small parties of motorists on the B1140 from one bank to the other Downstream a swing bridge that will be moved out of the way of river craft, but only during a 'window of opportunity' on this railway line to Lowestoft.
Tie up at Riverside.
Witton Green
Charming village on the dryer land behind Reedham.
Stop at Reedham Riverside. Walk uphill. Rail Station.
Berney Arms Mill (Tel: 01493 700605) (EH)
Boat or rail is the only access to the eponymous pub. The mill is seven storeys (70 foot) high and, after grinding cement clinker, was converted to drain the marshes (1870-1951). See the 24 foot diameter scoop wheel. Climb for the views.
Tie up by the pub or walk from Halvergate.

Start Points

3	Alexander Cruisers	
3	Alpha Craft	
3	Bees Boats	
3	Broom Boats Ltd	
3	Buccaneer Boats	
3	Fencraft	
3	Harbour Cruisers	
3	Silverline Marine	
3	Swan Craft	
3	VIP Harvey Eastwood	
4	Alpha Craft	
4	Castle Craft	
9	Anchorcraft	
9	Bridgecraft	
9	Horizon Craft	
25	Aston Boats	
25	H E Hipperson Ltd	
27	Barnes Brinkcraft	
27	Brister Craft	
27	Camelot Craft	
27	Connoisseur	
27	Faircraft Loyes	
27	Fineway Cruisers	
27	Moores & Co	
27	Royall and Son Ltd	
27	Sabena Marine	
27	Summercraft	
29	Belaugh Boats	
42	Broadland Riverine Boatcraft Ltd	

42	Maffett Cruisers
42	Pacific Cruisers Ltd
43	Broadwater Boats
43	Hunter Fleet
43	Ludham Marine
64	Eastwood Whelpton Ltd
69	Ferry Marina
69	Horning Pleasure Craft
69	King Line Cruisers
69	Norfolk Broads Yachting Company
69	Woods Dyke Boatyard Ltd
74	Hampton Boats Ltd
74	Topcraft Cruisers
75	Hearts Cruisers
75	Highcraft
75	Kingfisher Cruisers
76	Herbert Woods
76	Maycraft
86	Martham Boats
86	Martham Ferry Boatyard Ltd
98	Richardsons Cruisers
98	Rivercraft
101	Russell Marine
103	Sanderson Marine Craft Ltd
112	Sutton Staithe
127	Whispering Reeds

Wherry, Albion

Scotland

anals in Scotland are different. Two major routes were built to take masted sea-going craft between the east and west coasts with long lengths of lock free wide waterway without fixed bridges or tunnels. The few locks on the Caledonian Canal accept boats up to 160 long by 36 feet wide and are mainly in staircase formation. 39 locks on the Forth and Clyde Canal take boats 68 feet long by 20 feet wide but significantly there is a virtually lock free pound for 24 miles from Glasgow to Falkirk where it meets the Union Canal. One change in level then leads to the lock free 30 miles to Edinburgh.

Special boats were built to exploit these long distances of lock free travel. Initiated in Scotland these 'Swift boats' were pulled by teams of galloping horses and gave a fast smooth day and night service between the cities. Scotland also commissioned early steam engined boats, the first being the installation of a two-cylinder simple engine in the scow Thomas which gave out a 'puffing' exhaust. Many of these 'puffers' were built, one survives.

The reopening of the Forth and Clyde Canal (2001) allows sea-going yachts a circular route across the lowlands, through the Crinan Canal and into the Caledonian Canal, returning down the east coast.

Caledonian Canal and the Great Glen

Magnificent highlands, mysterious depths.

Caledonian Canal (1822)
Corpach - Neptune's Staircase - Moy - Gairlochy
Loch Lochy
Gairlochy - Ceann Loch - Laggan
Caledonian Canal (1822)
Laggan - Laggan Avenue - Laggan Swing Bridge
Loch Oich
Laggan Swing Bridge - Invergarry - Aberchalder
Caledonian Canal (1822)
Aberchalder - Cullochy - Kytra - Fort Augustus
Loch Ness
Fort Augustus - Invermoriston - Foyers - Urquhart Castle - Dores - Bona Lighthouse - Loch Dochfour

Caledonian Canal (1822)
Loch Dochfour - Dochgarroch - Muirtown - Clachnaharry

Allow 20 hours travel between limits for hire craft.
21 miles of wide canal, 38 miles of natural loch,
29 wide locks.
Seven Wonders: Neptune's Staircase

Combining expansive water travel with walks or cycle rides into the mountains makes for a perfect way to savour the natural grandeur of the glens.

Visitor attractions

Ben Nevis (4410 feet) (Britain's highest mountain.) Five hour walk to the top, a little less downhill, but the trail is a serious challenge, the weather uncertain. *Tie up in Fort William harbour. Take precautions.*

Neptune's Staircase Locks, Corpach

West Highland Museum
Highland memorabilia. Images of the exiled Bonnie Prince Charlie hidden in smears, only visible through mirrors. Other Jacobite rebellion artifacts.
Tie up in Fort William harbour.
Great Glen Cycle Route
Following the waterways for 80 miles, when not along the towpath, it winds through forests and along the hillsides.
Towpath lengths - Banavie to Gairlochy and Aberchalder to Fort Augustus / Loch Ness.
Glen Loy
River drains the Locheil Forest and passes under the canal on its largest aqueduct. Strone Viewpoint Walk (1 hour) and Errocht Oakwood Walk (1¾ hours).
Tie up east of the aqueduct. Both walks waymarked.
Well of Seven Heads
Chief Macdonnel revenged the murder of two of his sons (1663) by slaying the culprits and throwing their seven severed heads down this well. Monument erected 1812.
Tie up east of Laggan Swing Bridge, Loch Oich.
Inchnacardoch Forest
Across the River Oich, a huge forest with picnic sites and three waymarked walks. Nursery Walk (40 minutes), Pine Trees Walk (1 hour), River Walk (2 hours).
Tie up in Fort Augustus. Walk back one mile.
Loch Ness (24 miles long)
Tall mountains slope steeply down to 1000 feet below water level to create a water body larger than all the lakes of England and Wales put together. It has caught the imagination ever since a new road (1933) opened up the shoreline to passers by and a London surgeon purported to take a photograph of a 4 foot neck rising out of the water. Other 'sightings' (1960, 1979, 1987 and 1994) of the 'monster' have led to two exhibitions in Drumnadrochit which attempt to persuade visitors of the truth of the legend.
Tie up at Urquart Bay harbour.
John Cobb Memorial
His world water speed record attempt (1952) ended in disaster for John and his boat 'Crusader'.
Tie up at Strone Point, Loch Ness.
Urquhart Castle
Site of castle strongpoint for over 400 years. Robert the Bruce fought for it during the 13th century Wars of Independence. Jacobites laid siege (1689). Blown up to prevent rebel occupation, the silhouetted ruins are an enduring image of Loch Ness.
Tie up at Strone Point, Loch Ness.

Waterway distractions

Neptune's Staircase (64 feet rise)
Most spectacular set of eight locks (each 160 x 36 feet) built as one of three major staircases on the canal. Others are at Fort Augustus - set of five - and Muirtown - set of four. In the Highlands water supply was no problem.
East of the lock flight is limit of navigation for hire craft.
Strone Sluices
Main overflow when the Western Reach is filled with rain. Creates spectacular waterfall when in operation.
Tie up on the towpath west of Loy Aqueduct.
Moy Swing Bridge (1821)
Original Welsh-made cast iron, double-leaf swing bridge. All others now replaced (1930).
Tie up at either end.

Urquhart Castle and Loch Ness

Loch Oich (1858)

Summit of the crossing. Telford used a steam dredger to create a channel through two contiguous lochs. Ended up slightly shallower and narrower than the specifications elsewhere.
Take care to follow the channel markers.

Cherry Island

Artificial island made by piling stones on timber bed. A crannog built 3000 years ago, now uninhabited.
Tie up on the floating mooring alongside.

Falls of Foyers

Britain's first hydro-electric scheme (1896-1967) powered an aluminium smelter, using the drop of these falls (lower falls 90 feet and upper falls 30 feet).
Tie up in Foyers Bay, Loch Ness.

Muirtown Basin (2400 x 420 feet)

Massive excavation was needed to remove the ice-age deposits that blocked this outlet of the Glen.
British Waterways Canal Office. Winter moorings. Muirtown Top Wharf is hire craft limit of navigation.

ℹ️ Tourist Information

Fort William Tel: 01397 703781
Fort Augustus Tel: 01320 366367
Inverness Tel: 01463 234353

GEO Cruising Maps

GEOprojects: *Caledonian Canal and the Great Glen*

Start Points

48 Caley Cruisers Ltd   126 West Highland Sailing

Scotland 59

Forth & Clyde and Union Canals

Coast to coast and city to city.

Forth & Clyde Canal (1773, 1777, 1790-1963, 2001)
Bowling Basin - Dalmuir - Cloberhill Locks - Maryhill Locks - Stockingfield Jcn - Cadder - Kirkintilloch - Auchinstarry - Castlecary - Falkirk Wheel - River Carron
Union Canal (1822-1965, 2001)
Falkirk Wheel - Avon Aqueduct - Linlithgow - Almond Aqueduct - Wester Hailes - Edinburgh

Allow 26 hours travelling Bowling to Edinburgh plus time at the Falkirk Wheel.
64 miles of wide canal, 1 tunnel, 4 aqueducts, 27 wide locks.

Wide enough and deep enough for sea going yachts to pass from the Firth of Forth to the Clyde Estuary and for wide barges to go from Edinburgh to Glasgow. This newly re-opened pair of canals runs for many miles along the contours with only one major change of level at Falkirk (open 2002).

Visitor attractions

Saltings Nature Reserve, Bowling
Tidal flooding of grasslands encourages special species of orchids and insects. Man has added a living willow sculpture and a raised wooden walkway. Excellent.
Tie up in Bowling Basin.

Glasgow
Botanic gardens, Vaulted Cathedral, University, Hunterian Museum and Kelvingrove Museum.
Stop at Spiers Wharf - the end of the Glasgow Branch.

School of Art (1897-1909)
Simple bold masterpiece of architecture of the 'art nouveau' period. Charles Rennie Macintosh designed for his alma mater in superb detail - furniture and all.
Tie up near at Spiers Wharf. Go under motorway.

Cadder Churchyard - Burke and Hare
Medical science moves forward through research. Human organs were needed even in the 1820s. Cadder suffered from grave robbers and a vigil was kept over freshly buried bodies. A model of the movable shelter is found in the churchyard. Burke and Hare, canal labourers, lived in Edinburgh, murdered drunks and sold their bodies to Dr Knox, a local surgeon. The rumour that they came to Glasgow and transported corpses by boat to Edinburgh in chemical barrels is 'not proven'.
Tie up near Cadder Bridge.

Auld Kirk Museum, Kirkintilloch
Canal 'port', Roman artifacts, build a 'Kirky Puffer'.
Tie up at Townhead Bridge.

Antonine Wall (AD142, 37 miles)
Roman defence against marauding Scots was of turf on a stone base with a 40 foot ditch in front and peppered with forts - canalside at Tintock, on Bar Hill Twechar, south of Craigmarloch and many other places. The best preserved is at Rough Castle.
Tie up at Tinlock, Twechar Bridge, Criaigmarloch Bridge and Bonnybridge Lifting Bridge. Short walks.

Callendar House and Park (Tel: 01324 503770)
The owner refused to allow the canal to pass through his grounds thus forcing the construction of Scotland's only waterway tunnel. House now open, with staff in period costume. Interactive exhibits

celebrate Falkirk from Jacobian times to the railway age. Archive in History Research Centre.
Tie up at Walkers Bridge. Long walk northeast (B803).

Linlithgow Palace and Loch (Tel: 01506 842896)
'Princely Palace' overlooks the loch. Birthplace of Mary Queen of Scots, residence of the Stewart Kings.
Tie up east of Manse Rd. Bridge. Summer boat trips.

Edinburgh - Old and New Towns
Old city crowded on the shoulders of the rock and the Georgian layout of wide streets and squares have both been accorded World Heritage status. Hundreds of buildings are listed as important, Royal Museum of Scotland is the freshest of many monuments and museums that adorn the City.
   Annual International Arts Festival in the autumn.
Tie up at the terminus.

Edinburgh Castle
Standing at the head of The Royal Mile, this most famous of many city attractions, houses the major symbol of Scottish Sovereignty - The Stone of Destiny, as well as the Crown Jewels of Scotland.
Tie up at the terminus.

Royal Yacht 'Britannia'
Built in Scotland, moored on Leith waterfront. Tread in the footsteps of Kings and Queens.
Tie up at the terminus.

Waterway distractions

Dalmuir Drop Lock (apparent clearance 20 inches)
Close both sets of gates, pump out the water and boats have 10 foot extra clearance. Pass under a road bridge.
Follow lock keeper's instructions. 20 minute cycle.

Maryhill Locks
Continuous stonework from the Kelvin Aqueduct past five exaggerated goblet shaped side pounds to the start of the 13 mile summit level makes these five locks a most impressive feature.
Tie up at either end of the aqueduct.

Fishing boat, Auchinstarry

Dullatur Bog, Kilsyth
Messy mire conquered by navvies shovelling tons of earth and stones into the bog - 50 feet deep.
Observe the width of the cut.

Lock 16, Port Downie (1809, 1822-1848)
Top of the sixteen locks down to the River Carron and the Firth of Forth. Terminal basin of horse-drawn day and night passenger services on the 'Swift boats' from Glasgow. Overlooked by the Georgian Union Inn. Onward passage to Edinburgh was by horse-drawn stagecoach until the 31 mile Edinburgh and Glasgow Union Canal arrived down their only lock flight (11 locks filled in 1933).
Make a short detour before entering the modern

replacement for the lock flight - the Falkirk Wheel.

Falkirk Tunnel
Built to hide the canal from Callendar House.
Towpath with handrail passes through this once dark
tunnel. See stalactites formed over the last 180 years.
Tie up near Glen Bridge 61.

Glen Bridge
Keystones show faces 'Laughin' and 'Greetin'. Much
photographed.
Tie up near Glen Bridge 61.

Avon Aqueduct (1858)
12 arched and longest and highest of Scotland's
aqueducts which preserved the single contour of the
Union Canal.
Tie up at Bridge 48.

Leamington Lift Bridge
'Four poster' lift bridge at the entrance to Lochrin
Basin was formerly located at Fountainbridge.
Tie up in the basin.

Worth a detour

Glasgow Branch
Overhead waterway to Hamiltonhill Basin and Spiers
Wharf. View work by Charles Rennie Macintosh.
2 miles, 0 locks each way. Allow 2 hours.

ℹ️ *Tourist Information*
Glasgow Tel: 0141 204 4400
Falkirk Tel: 01324 620244
Linlithgow Tel: 01506 844600
Edinburgh Tel: 0131 473 3800

GEO *Cruising Maps*
GEOprojects: *Forth & Clyde and Union Canals with
the Crinan Canal*

Start Points
116 Thistle Boats

Falkirk Wheel

Falkirk Wheel (2002)
Latest European boat lift, in the form of the world's first rotating boat lift, will be open for use in Spring 2002. It
will complement the world's first ever boat lift (1875) erected at Anderton, Cheshire, also to a British design.

Restoring the connection between the Union Canal and the coast to coast Forth and Clyde Canal 112 feet below,
it will take 15 minutes for each cycle and replaces a flight of eleven locks (1822-1933) which took so long for
boats to negotiate that passengers in the old 'Swift boats' used to walk down a special path to meet a second boat
in Port Downie Basin below.

Massive and elegant, the 115 feet diameter two-arm wheel will be visible for miles around. The end of each arm
will have 80 tonne gondolas, each carrying four boats in a ¼ of a million litres of water - a total of 1800 tonnes.
Boats will approach from above via a new section of canal which tunnels under the ancient Roman Antonine Wall
and then across an aqueduct to the upper level of the wheel. From below, two locks will give entry to a 20 boat
holding basin at the lower level of the wheel. Public access to ride the wheel will be along the aqueduct at the top
and by a trip boat from the bottom. A massive reflective glassed visitor centre will provide a weather protected
vantage point to see the action and will host corporate meetings or school parties with ease by day and night.
www.millenniumlink.org.uk has live web-cam images of the site.

Regional Maps

Map Reference

Broad Canal (over 7ft wide)
- —— Navigable
- ≡ No longer navigable
- ═ Under restoration

Narrow Canal (max 7ft wide)
- —— Navigable
- ≡ No longer navigable
- ═ Under restoration

River Navigation
- ···· Navigable
- ≡ No longer navigable
- ═ Under restoration

Tidal River Navigation
- —— Navigable
- ≡ No longer navigable
- ═ Under restoration

Other Navigation
- ≡ Canal with lock size unknown
- ┈┈ Proposed navigation

- ⌒ Other river
- ⬭ Built-up area
- ━━ National boundary
- ⅄ Lock flight with number of locks
- ▣ Tunnel
- ◢ Inclined plane
- ◇ Feature of interest
- ⚠ Local hazard
- ○ 12M / 8L ○ Distance in miles/number of locks between markers
- ◣ 80 Height of waterway in feet above sea-level

Scale 1: 700 000

| 0 | 10 | 20 | 30 miles |

| 0 | 10 | 20 | 30 | 40 | 50 kilometres |

ILFRACOMBE

Bris

_E_

BRAUNTON
Braunton Canal

BARNSTAPLE

Barnstaple or Bideford Bay

NORTHAM
River Torridge

BIDEFORD

WEARE GIFFARD
◇ **Beam (Torridge) Aqueduct**
Torrington (Rolle) Canal
GREAT TORRINGTON
◣ 70

Tamar Lakes
4½M / 0L ◣ 430 VIRWORTHY
Virworthy Branch
Brendon Moor Junction

Hobbacott Down Incline
3½M / 0L
VENN
BLAGDONMOOR WHARE

Bude Bay
BUDE
1¼M / 1L
HELEBRIDGE
◇ 380
Red Post Junction
6½M / 0L
HOLSWORTHY

4M / 2L

Bude Canal
Druxton Branch

NORTH TAMERTON
16M / 0L

210 ◣ DRUXTON

OKEHAMPTON

BOSCASTLE

CAMELFORD

LAUNCESTON

Torridge

Taw

BODMIN MOOR

PADSTOW
Camel
Allen
Camel

WADEBRIDGE

BODMIN

TRENANCE
St Columb Canal
WHITEWATER FARM
◣ 200
ST COLUMB MAJOR

LUSTY GLAZE
NEWQUAY
RIALTON BARTON

Fowey

DARTMOOR

TWO BRIDGES

East Dart

Mill Hill Branch
MILL HILL
TAVISTOCK
GUNNISLAKE
Tavistock Canal
Tamar Manure Navigation
◇ **Morwellham Quay & Incline**

River Tamar
Tavy

160
MOORSWATER
LISKEARD
Liskeard & Looe Union Canal
SANDPLACE
LOOE
River Looe

LOSTWITHIEL
River Fowey
PONTS MILL
◣ 30
ST BLAZEY
Par Canal
PAR
7M / 0L
FOWEY

9M / 0L
SALTASH
CRABTREE
Cann Quarry Canal
PLYMOUTH
River Plym
IVYBRIDGE
Plym
Erme

PERRANPORTH

TRURO
Truro River
REDRUTH

ST IVES
CAMBORNE
Hayle or Copperhouse Canal
HAYLE

Fal
River Fal
MEVAGISSEY

Allen

PENZANCE

FALMOUTH

HELSTON
Cober

Mount's Bay

A   B   C

In most cases the canal and river navigations shown in this section of maps have been at one time authorised as navigations by private Act of Parliament. This gives a statutory right of navigation generally to pleasure craft and mechanically powered boats. Canals classed as 'under restoration' are those which are actively being restored.

The classification of canals under either Broad of Narrow refers to the width of the locks the canal was built with, dictated by the type of craft intending to use the canal:

Narrow canals were built for narrowboats which normally had a standard 7ft beam, were up to 70ft long with a capacity of 20-30 tons.

Broad canals are generally designed to accomodate craft that plied on the rivers to which they connect. The locks therefore catered for boats of 14ft beam and with a length of 52ft to 72ft.

Scale 1: 825 000

0   10   20   30 miles

0 10 20 30 40 50 kilometres

JURA

CRINAN
Summit
Level
64
5   4   9M
15L
LOCHGILPHEAD
Crinan Canal
ARDRISHAIG

BUTE

ARRAN

TAYINLOAN

MACHRIHANISH   20   CAMPBELTOWN
Campbeltown
Canal

GARELOCHHEAD

HELENSBURGH
BALLOCH
ALEXANDRIA
DUNOON
GREENOCK
PORT
GLASGOW
DUMBARTON
BOWLING
CLYDEBANK
WEMYSS BAY

TARBERT

ROTHESAY

LARGS

KILBIRNIE

ARDROSSAN
SALTCOATS
STEVENSTON
Stevenston Canal   40
IRVINE
TROON
PRESTWICK
AYR

STEWARTON

KILMARNOCK
Irvine
DARVEL

STRATHAVEN

DALMELLINGTON

GIRVAN

BALLANTRAE

STRANRAER
GLENLUCE

NEWTON STEWART
CREETOWN
WIGTOWN

WHITHORN

Luce Bay

Wigtown
Bay

DRYMEN
Endrick Water
FINTRY
STRATHBLANE
River Leven
30
2½M
0L
KIRKINTILLOCH
7½M
0L
Kelvin
Aqueduct
Stockingfield Junction
MARYHILL
Glasgow Branch
RENFREW
Forth & Cart Junction Canal
Cart Navigation
PAISLEY
JOHNSTONE
Glasgow, Paisley &
Johnstone Canal
19½M
0L
50L
5
RUTHERGLEN
PORT EGLINTON
30
GLASGOW
BARRHEAD
NEWTON
MEARNS
EAST
KILBRIDE
HAMILTON
MOTHERWELL
WISHAW
LARKHALL
CARLUKE

STIRLING
KENNET PANS
14½M
0L
4M
15L
River
Carron
CAMELON
DENNY
BANKNOCK
KILSYTH
Summit Level 160
NETHERWOOD
Glassford's
Cut
CUMBERNAULD
22M
4L
Falkirk
Wheel
130
160
Monkland Basin
Monkland Canal
COATBRIDGE
AIRDRIE
CALDERBANK
260
CAMBUSLANG
BELLSHILL
GARTSHERRIE

River Forth
TILLICOULTRY
ALLOA
KILBAGIE
Kilbagie Canal
10L
KINCARDINE
GRANGEMOUTH
BO'NESS
Bo'ness Canal
LINLITHGOW
FALKIRK
11
Port
Maxwell
Branch
250
12M
3L
Avon
Aqueduct
Linlithgow Union
Canal Society
Museum
Union Canal
Edinburgh & Glasgow Union
LIVINGSTON
WHITBURN
1 Calder Branch
2 Dundyvan Branch
3 Langloan Branch

COWDENBEATH
DUNFERMLINE
INVERKE
QUEENS
22M
0L
BROXBURN
WESTER HAI

FORTH
LANARK
BIGGAR

MUIRKIRK
Muirkirk Canal

CUMNOCK

SANQUHAR

THORNHILL

MONIAIVE

NEW GALLOWAY   150

Clatteringshaws
Loch

Loch Ken

GLENLOCHAR
Carlingwark
Canal
CASTLE DOUGLAS
Carlingwark
Lane
Carlingwark Loch

GATEHOUSE
OF FLEET
Water of Fleet
TONGLAND
KIRKCUDBRIGHT

DUMFRIES
River Nith
CAERLAVEROCK

LOCHMABEN   LOCKERBIE
MOFFAT

SOUTHERN UPL

SILLOTH

Solway Firth

MARYPORT

WORKINGTON   River Derwent   130   COCKERM
WHITEHAVEN
EGREMONT
SEASCALE

72

A   B   C

D   E   F

Moray Firth

1

LOSSIEMOUTH
FRASERBURGH

BUCKIE
BANFF

ELGIN

North Ugie Water
ST FERGUS
RORA
FORRES
Spey
Deveron
KEITH
Isla
TURRIFF
South Ugie Water
60
Pitfour Canal
NAIRN
Ugie
INVERUGIE
PETERHEAD

Dorback Burn
CHARLESTOWN OF
ABERLOUR
HUNTLY
Deveron
ELLON

2

Yrhan
OLDMELDRUM

GRANTOWN-ON-SPEY

INVERURIE
PORT ELPHINSTONE
Avon
160
KINTORE
Don
Aberdeenshire Canal
DYCE
AVIEMORE
TOMINTOUL
Luineag Loch Morlich
ALFORD
Don
ABERDEEN

COCK BRIDGE

U N T A I N S

BALLATER
Dee
BANCHORY
Dee
BRAEMAR

STONEHAVEN

3

North Esk

BLAIR ATHOLL

Shee Water

S T R A T H M O R E

PITLOCHRY
Tummel
Blackwater
BRECHIN
MONTROSE
Tay
Isla
South Esk
KIRRIEMUIR
ABERFELDY
BLAIRGOWRIE
Ericht
FORFAR
Isla
COUPAR
ANGUS
ARBROATH
STANLEY
Dighty Water
CARNOUSTIE
Tay
Almond
DUNDEE
CRIEFF
TAYPORT
30
6½M
PERTH
0L
Perth Town Lode
River Tay
Firth of Tay

Earn
BRIDGE OF EARN
River Earn
NEWBURGH
ST ANDREWS
AUCHTERARDER
6M
Eden
CUPAR
0L
O C H I L H I L L S
BURNTURK
320
CRAIL
KINGSKETTLE
Burnturk Canals
KINROSS
Sir Andrew Wood's Canal
160
UPPER LARGO
Leven Loch Leven LEVEN
TILLICOULTRY
GLENROTHES
BUCKHAVEN

r Forth
ALLOA
10
KILBAGIE
COWDENBEATH
KIRKCALDY
INET PANS
Kilbagie Canal
KINCARDINE
DUNFERMLINE
4M
15L
River Carron
D   E   F
NORTH BERWICK
h of Forth

4

74 75
72 73
70 71
66 67 68 69
62 63 64 65

Scale 1: 825 000

| 0 | 10 | 20 | 30 miles |

| 0 | 10 | 20 | 30 | 40 | 50 kilometres |

Hirebases

Adelaide Marine Ltd   17 **1**
Broxbourne, Lee Navigation
Tel: 01992 462085, www.adelaidemarine.com

Adelaide Marine Ltd   8, 14, 17, 45 **2**
Norwood Green, Grand Union Canal
Tel: 020 8571 5678, www.adelaidemarine.com

Alexander Cruisers   57 **3**
Brundall, River Yare
Tel: 01603 715048, www.alexandercruisers.co.uk

Alpha Craft   57 **3**
Brundall, River Yare
Tel: 01603 713265,
www.norfolkbroads.com/alphacraft

Alpha Craft   57 **4**
St Olaves, River Waveney
Tel: 01603 713265,
www.norfolkbroads.com/alphacraft

Alvechurch Boat Centres   22, 26, 34 **5**
Alvechurch, Worcester and Birmingham Canal
Tel: 0121 445 2909, www.alvechurch.com

Alvechurch Boat Centres   46, 48 **6**
Gayton, Grand Union Canal
Tel: 0121 445 2909, www.alvechurch.com

Alvechurch Boat Centres   29, 41 **7**
Northwich, Trent and Mersey Canal
Tel: 0121 445 2909, www.alvechurch.com

Alvechurch Boat Centres   12, 41 **8**
Wrenbury, Llangollen Canal
Tel: 0121 445 2909, www.alvechurch.com

Anchorcraft   57 **9**
Acle, River Bure
Tel: 01493 750500

Andersen Boats   11, 12, 29, 41 **10**
Middlewich, Trent and Mersey Canal
Tel: 01606 833668, www.andersenboats.com

Anglo Welsh Waterway Holidays   36 **11**
Bath, Kennet and Avon Canal
Tel: 0117 924 1200, www.anglowelsh.co.uk

Anglo Welsh Waterway Holidays   36 **12**
Bristol, Kennet and Avon Canal
Tel: 0117 924 1200, www.anglowelsh.co.uk

Anglo Welsh Waterway Holidays   12, 41 **13**
Bunbury, Shropshire Union Canal
Tel: 0117 924 1200, www.anglowelsh.co.uk

Anglo Welsh Waterway Holidays   22, 41 **14**
Great Haywood, Staffordshire and Worcestershire Canal
Tel: 0117 924 1200, www.anglowelsh.co.uk

Anglo Welsh Waterway Holidays   6, 46 **15**
Lower Heyford, Oxford Canal
Tel: 0117 924 1200, www.anglowelsh.co.uk

Anglo Welsh Waterway Holidays   29, 33, 53 **16**
New Mills, Peak Forest Canal
Tel: 0117 924 1200, www.anglowelsh.co.uk

Anglo Welsh Waterway Holidays   41 **17**
Norbury, Shropshire Union Canal
Tel: 0117 924 1200, www.anglowelsh.co.uk

Anglo Welsh Waterway Holidays   22, 26, 34 **18**
Tardebigge, Worcester and Birmingham Canal
Tel: 0117 924 1200, www.anglowelsh.co.uk

Anglo Welsh Waterway Holidays   12 **19**
Trevor, Llangollen Canal
Tel: 0117 924 1200, www.anglowelsh.co.uk

Anglo Welsh Waterway Holidays   12 **20**
Welshpool, Montgomery Canal
Tel: 0117 924 1200, www.anglowelsh.co.uk

Anglo Welsh Waterway Holidays   34, 39 **21**
Wootton Wawen, Stratford-upon-Avon Canal

Tel: 0117 924 1200, www.anglowelsh.co.uk

Arlen Hire Boats   16, 50 **22**
Preston, Lancaster Canal
Tel: 01772 769183, www.arlen-hireboats.co.uk

Ashby Boat Company   31, 39 **23**
Stoke Golding, Ashby Canal
Tel: 01455 212671, www.ashbyboats.co.uk

Aspley Wharf Marina   33, 53 **24**
Huddersfield, Huddersfield Narrow / Broad Canal
Tel: 01484 514123

Aston Boats   57 **25**
Beccles, River Waveney
Tel: 01502 713960,
www.norfolkbroads.com/astonboats

Avalon Narrowboat Co   6, 46 **26**
Enslow, Oxford Canal
Tel: 01285 750567, www.avalonboats.com

Barnes Brinkcraft   57 **27**
Wroxham, River Bure
Tel: 01603 782625 / 782333,
www.barnesbrinkcraft.co.uk

Beacon Park Boats   20 **28**
Llanfoist, Monmouthshire and Brecon Canal
Tel: 01873 858277, www.beaconparkboats.com

Bees Boats   57 **3**
Brundall, River Yare
Tel: 01603 713446, www.beesboats.co.uk

Belaugh Boats   57 **29**
Belaugh, River Bure
Tel: 01603 782802,
www.norfolkbroads.com/belaughboats

Berry Brook Boats   37, 45 **30**
Reading, River Thames
Tel: 01491 579447, www.berrybrookboats.co.uk

Bidford Boats   26, 34 **31**
Bidford-on-Avon, River Avon
Tel: 01789 773205, www.bidfordboats.co.uk

Black Prince Holidays   29, 41, 50 **32**
Acton Bridge, Trent and Mersey Canal
Tel: 01527 575115, www.black-prince.com

Black Prince Holidays   12 **33**
Chirk, Llangollen Canal
Tel: 01527 575115, www.black-prince.com

Black Prince Holidays   53 **34**
Silsden, Leeds and Liverpool Canal
Tel: 01527 575115, www.black-prince.com

Black Prince Holidays   11, 29, 41 **35**
Stoke-on-Trent, Trent and Mersey Canal
Tel: 01527 575115, www.black-prince.com

Black Prince Holidays   9, 22, 26, 34 **36**
Stoke Prior, Worcester and Birmingham Canal
Tel: 01527 575115, www.black-prince.com

Blisworth Tunnel Boats Ltd   46, 48 **37**
Blisworth, Grand Union Canal
Tel: 01604 858868, www.blisworthtunnel.co.uk

Blisworth Tunnel Boats Ltd   31 **38**
Shardlow, Trent and Mersey Canal
Tel: 01332 792271, www.blisworthtunnel.co.uk

Bridge Boats Ltd   37, 45 **39**
Reading, River Thames
Tel: 0118 959 0346, www.bridgeboats.com

Bridge Boatyard   49 **40**
Ely, Great Ouse Navigation
Tel: 01353 663726, www.bridgeboatyard.com

Bridgecraft   57 **9**
Acle, River Bure
Tel: 01493 750378

Bridgewater Boats   45 **41**
Berkhamsted, Grand Union Canal

Tel: 01442 863615, www.bridgewater-boats.co.uk

Brister Craft   57 **27**
Wroxham, River Bure
Tel: 01603 783783,
www.norfolkbroads.co.uk/bristercraft

Broadland Riverine Boatcraft Ltd   57 **42**
Loddon, River Chet
Tel: 01508 528735

Broadwater Boats   57 **43**
Ludham, River Thurne
Tel: 01692 678040

Brook Line Narrowboat Holidays   9, 26, 34 **44**
Dunhampstead, Worcester and Birmingham Canal
Tel: 01905 773889

Broom Boats Ltd   57 **3**
Brundall, River Yare
Tel: 01603 712334, www.broom-boats.co.uk

Bruce Charitable Trust   36 **45**
Devizes, Kennet and Avon Canal
Tel: 01672 515498, www.brucetrust.org.uk

Bruce Charitable Trust   37 **46**
Great Bedwyn, Kennet and Avon Canal
Tel: 01672 515498, www.brucetrust.org.uk

Buccaneer Boats   57 **3**
Brundall, River Yare
Tel: 01603 712057

Calcutt Boats Ltd   31, 39, 46 **47**
Napton-on-the-Hill, Grand Union Canal
Tel: 01926 813757 / 812075, www.calcuttboats.com

Caley Cruisers Ltd   59 **48**
Inverness, Caledonian Canal
Tel: 01463 236328, www.caleycruisers.co.uk

Cambrian Cruisers   20 **49**
Pencelli, Monmouthshire and Brecon Canal
Tel: 01874 665313, www.cambriancruisers.co.uk

Camelot Craft   57 **27**
Wroxham, River Bure
Tel: 01603 783096, www.camelotcraft.co.uk

Canalboat Holidays Ltd   31, 39, 46 **50**
Weedon Bec, Grand Union Canal
Tel: 01327 340739, www.canalboat-holidays.co.uk

Canal Cruising Company Ltd   11, 41 **51**
Stone, Trent and Mersey Canal
Tel: 01785 813982, www.canalcruising.co.uk

Castle Craft   57 **4**
St Olaves, River Waveney
Tel: 01493 488675

Castle Narrowboats   20 **52**
Gilwern, Monmouthshire and Brecon Canal
Tel: 01873 830001,
www.canaljunction.com/castlenarrowboats

Caversham Boat Services   37, 45 **39**
Reading, River Thames
Tel: 0118 957 4323, www.caveshamboat.co.uk

Chas. Hardern & Co   12, 41 **53**
Beeston, Shropshire Union Canal
Tel: 01829 732595, www.chashardern.co.uk

Chertsey Meads Marine (Hire)   14, 24, 45 **130**
Chertsey, River Thames
Tel: 01932 564699

Cheshire Cat Narrowboat Hire   12, 29, 41 **54**
Cholmondeston, Shropshire Union Canal
Tel: 01274 884094,
www.canaljunction.com/cheshirecat

Claymoore Navigation Ltd   29, 33, 41, 50 **55**
Preston Brook, Bridgewater Canal
Tel: 01928 717273, www.claymoore.co.uk

Clifton Cruisers   31, 39 **56**
Rugby, Oxford Canal

Tel: 08707 451164, www.canalia.com/clifton.cruisers
Club Line Cruisers   31, 39 **57**
Coventry, Coventry Canal
Tel: 024 7625 8864
College Cruisers   6, 46 **58**
Oxford, Oxford Canal
Tel: 01865 554343, www.collegecruisers.com
Connoisseur   57 **27**
Wroxham, River Bure
Tel: 01603 782472, www.connoisseurafloat.com
Constellation Cruises Ltd   29, 33, 41, 53 **59**
Higher Poynton, Macclesfield Canal
Tel: 01625 873471
Copt Heath Wharf   22, 26, 34, 39 **60**
Catherine-de-Barnes, Grand Union Canal
Tel: 0121 704 4464, www.copteathwharf.co.uk
Coronet Canal Carrying Co   31, 39 **61**
North Kilworth, Grand Union Canal, Leicester Line
Tel: 01788 510410, www.coronet-canal.co.uk
Cotswold Boat Hire   6 **91**
Lechlade, River Thames
Tel: 01793 700241
Country Craft Narrowboats   20 **62**
Llangynidr, Monmouthshire and Brecon Canal
Tel: 01874 730850, www.country-craft.co.uk
Countrywide Cruisers   18, 22, 34, 41 **63**
Brewood, Shropshire Union Canal
Tel: 01902 850166, www.countrywide-cruisers.com
Eastwood Whelpton Ltd   57 **64**
Upton, River Bure
Tel: 01493 750430,
www.norfolkbroads.com/whelpton
Empress Holidays Ltd   12, 29, 41 **65**
Nantwich, Shropshire Union Canal
Tel: 01270 624075, www.empressholidays.com
Evesham Marina Holidays   26, 34 **66**
Evesham, River Avon
Tel: 01386 48906
Faircraft Loyes   57 **27**
Wroxham, River Bure
Tel: 01603 782207, www.broads.co.uk
Farncombe Boat House   24 **67**
Godalming, River Wey
Tel: 01483 421306, www.farncombeboats.co.uk
Fencraft   57 **3**
Brundall, River Yare
Tel: 01603 715011
Ferryline Cruisers   14, 24, 45 **68**
Thames Ditton, River Thames
Tel: 020 8398 0271 / 2
Ferry Marina   57 **69**
Horning, River Bure
Tel: 01692 630692, www.ferryboats.co.uk
Fineway Cruisers   57 **27**
Wroxham, River Bure
Tel: 01603 782309, www.finewayleisure.co.uk
Fox Boats   49 **70**
March, Middle Level Navigation
Tel: 01354 652770, www.foxboats.co.uk
Foxhangers Canal Holidays   36 **45**
Devizes, Kennet and Avon Canal
Tel: 01380 828795, www.foxhangers.co.uk
Foxton Boat Services Ltd   31 **71**
Foxton, Grand Union Canal, Leicester Line
Tel: 0116 279 2285, www.foxtonboats.co.uk
Galleon Marine   24 **72**
Odiham, Basingstoke Canal
Tel: 01256 703691, www.galleonmarine.co.uk
Guildford Boat House Ltd   24 **73**

Guildford, River Wey
Tel: 01483 504494, www.guildfordboats.co.uk
H E Hipperson Ltd   57 **25**
Beccles, River Waveney
Tel: 01502 712166
Hampton Boats Ltd   57 **74**
Oulton Broad, River Waveney
Tel: 01502 572036
Harbour Cruisers   57 **3**
Brundall, River Yare
Tel: 01603 712146, www.norfolkbroads.com/harbour
Hearts Cruisers   57 **75**
Thorpe St Andrew, River Yare
Tel: 01603 433666
Herbert Woods   57 **76**
Potter Heigham, River Thurne
Tel: 01692 670711, www.broads.co.uk
Heritage Narrowboats   11, 29, 41 **77**
Scholar Green, Macclesfield Canal
Tel: 01782 785700, www.sherbornewharf.co.uk
Highcraft   57 **75**
Thorpe St Andrew, River Yare
Tel: 01603 701701
Horizon Craft   57 **9**
Acle, River Bure
Tel: 01493 750283
Horning Pleasure Craft   57 **69**
Horning, River Bure
Tel: 01692 630128
Hunter Fleet   57 **43**
Ludham, The Thurne
Tel: 01692 678263, www.huntersyard.co.uk
Ian Goode Narrowboats   31 **78**
Kibworth Beauchamp, Grand Union Canal, Leicester
Line
Tel: 0116 279 3034
Jannel Cruisers Ltd   22, 31 **79**
Burton upon Trent, Trent and Mersey Canal
Tel: 01283 542718, www.jannel.co.uk
Kate Boats Warwick   26, 31, 39 **80**
Warwick, Grand Union Canal
Tel: 01926 492968, www.kateboats.co.uk
Kennet Cruises   37, 45 **81**
Reading, Kennet and Avon Canal
Tel: 0118 987 1115, www.kennetcruises.co.uk
Kingcraft   6, 46 **82**
Abingdon, River Thames
Tel: 01235 521125
Kingfisher Cruisers   57 **75**
Thorpe St Andrew, River Yare
Tel: 01603 437682, www.outofthegloom.com/dad
King Line Cruisers   57 **69**
Horning, River Bure
Tel: 01692 630297, www.norfolk-broads.co.uk
Kris Cruisers   24, 45 **83**
Datchet, River Thames
Tel: 01753 543930, www.kriscruisers.co.uk
London & Home Counties Narrowboat
Holidays   31, 39 **57**
Coventry, Coventry Canal
Tel: 01926 864156,
www.london-narrowboat-holidays.com
London & Home Counties Narrowboat
Holidays   8, 14, 17, 45 **2**
Norwood Green, River Thames
Tel: 01926 864156,
www.london-narrowboat-holidays.com
London & Home Counties Narrowboat
Holidays   37, 45 **30**

Reading, River Thames
Tel: 01926 864156,
www.london-narrowboat-holidays.com
Lower Park Marina   50, 53 **84**
Barnoldswick, Leeds and Liverpool Canal
Tel: 01282 815883
Ludham Marine   57 **43**
Ludham, River Thurne
Tel: 01493 678322
Maestermyn Cruisers   12 **85**
Whittington, Llangollen Canal
Tel: 01691 662424, www.maestermyn.co.uk
Maffett Cruisers   57 **42**
Loddon, River Chet
Tel: 01508 520344
Marine Services   12 **33**
Chirk, Llangollen Canal
Tel: 01691 774558, www.chirkmarina.com
Martham Boats   57 **86**
Martham, River Thurne
Tel: 01493 740249, www.marthanboats.com
Martham Ferry Boatyard Ltd   57 **86**
Martham, River Thurne
Tel: 01493 740303
Maycraft   57 **76**
Potter Heigham, River Thurre
Tel: 01692 670241
Middlewich Narrowboats   11, 12, 29, 41 **10**
Middlewich, Trent and Mersey Canal
Tel: 01606 832460, www.middlewichboats.co.uk
Montgomery Canal Cruises   12 **20**
Welshpool, Montgomery Canal
Tel: 01938 553271 / 554979, www.montycanal.co.uk
Moonraker Narrowboats   36 **87**
Trowbridge, Kennet and Avon Canal
Tel: 01787 473599, www.moonraker.co.uk
Moores & Co   57 **27**
Wroxham, River Bure
Tel: 01603 783311, www.boatingholidays.co.uk
Napton Narrowboats   31, 46, 39 **88**
Napton-on-the-Hill, Oxford Canal
Tel: 01926 813644, www.napton-marina.co.uk
Nationwide Narrowboats   48 **89**
Bedford, River Great Ouse
Tel: 01525 874335
www.canaljunction.com/nationwide
Nationwide Narrowboats   45, 48 **90**
Bletchley, Grand Union Canal
Tel: 01525 874335
www.canaljunction.com/nationwide
Norfolk Broads Yachting Company   57 **69**
Horning, River Bure
Tel: 01692 631330, www.norfolk-broads.com
Oxfordshire Narrowboats   6, 46 **15**
Lower Heyford, Oxford Canal
Tel: 01869 340348
www.oxfordshire-narrowboats.co.uk
Pacific Cruisers Ltd   57 **42**
Loddon, River Chet
Tel: 01508 520321
www.norfolkbroads.com/pacificcruisers
Peak Forest Cruisers   29, 41 **92**
Macclesfield, Macclesfield Canal
Tel: 01625 424172
Pegary Boat Hire   22, 26, 34, 39 **93**
Majors Green, Stratford-upon-Avon Canal
Tel: 0121 474 6388, www.pegary.demon.co.uk
Pennine Cruisers   50, 53 **94**
Skipton, Leeds and Liverpool Canal

Tel: 01756 795478, www.penninecruisers.com

Reading Marine Company   **37, 45** 95
Padworth, Kennet and Avon Canal
Tel: 0118 971 3666, www.readingmarine.com

Red Line Boats   **20** 96
Llanover, Monmouthshire and Brecon Canal
Tel: 01873 880516, www.redlineboats.co.uk

Red Line Cruisers   **6, 46** 97
Eynsham, River Thames
Tel: 01865 882542, www.redlinecruisers.com

Richardsons Cruisers   **57** 98
Stalham, River Ant
Tel: 01692 581081

Rivercraft   **57** 98
Stalham, River Ant
Tel: 01692 580288, www.broadland.com/rivercraft

Road House Narrowboats   **20** 99
Gilwern, Monmouthshire and Brecon Canal
Tel: 01873 830240

Rose Narrowboats Ltd   **31, 39** 100
Stretton under Fosse, Oxford Canal
Tel: 01788 832449, www.roseboat.demon.co.uk

Royall and Son Ltd   **57** 27
Wroxham, River Bure
Tel: 01603 782743,
www.norfolkbroads.com/royallandson

Russell Marine   **57** 101
South Walsham, River Bure
Tel: 01603 270262

Sabena Marine   **57** 27
Wroxham, River Bure
Tel: 01603 782552, www.sabenamarine.co.uk

Sally Boats   **36** 102
Bradford-on-Avon, Kennet and Avon Canal
Tel: 01225 864923, www.sallyboats.ltd.uk

Sanderson Marine Craft Ltd   **57** 103
Reedham, River Yare
Tel: 01493 700242,
www.norfolkbroads.com/sandersonmarine

Shepley Bridge Marina Ltd   **33, 53** 104
Mirfield, Calder and Hebble Navigation
Tel: 01924 491872, www.shepleybridgemarina.com

Sherborne Wharf   **18, 22, 26, 34, 39** 105
Birmingham, Birmingham Canal Navigations
Tel: 0121 455 6163, www.sherbornewharf.co.uk

Shire Cruisers   **33, 50, 53** 106
Sowerby Bridge, Rochdale Canal / Calder and
Hebble Navigation
Tel: 01422 832712, www.shirecruisers.co.uk

Sileby Mill Boatyard   **31** 107
Sileby, Soar Navigation
Tel: 01509 813583, www.silebymill.co.uk

Silsden Boats   **53** 34
Silsden, Leeds and Liverpool Canal
Tel: 01535 653675, www.silsdenboats.co.uk

Silverline Marine   **57** 3
Brundall, River Yare
Tel: 01603 712247

Snaygill Boats Ltd   **50, 53** 108
Low Bradley, Leeds and Liverpool Canal
Tel: 01756 795150, www.snaygillboats.co.uk

Starline Narrowboats   **9, 26, 34** 109
Upton upon Severn, River Severn
Tel: 01684 574774, www.starline.demon.co.uk

Stroudwater Cruisers   **9, 26, 34** 110
Stourport-on-Severn, Staffordshire and
Worcestershire Canal / River Severn
Tel: 01299 877222, www.stroudwater-cruisers.co.uk

Summercraft   **57** 27

Wroxham, River Bure
Tel: 01603 782809

Sunset Hoildays   **36** 111
Limpley Stoke, Kennet and Avon Canal
Tel: 01249 730850, www.sunsetholidays.com

Sutton Staithe   **57** 112
Sutton, River Ant
Tel: 01692 581653,
www.norfolkbroads.com/suttonstaithe

Swancraft Boat Services Ltd   **45, 46** 131
Benson, River Thames
Tel: 01491 836700

Swan Craft   **57** 3
Brundall, River Yare
Tel: 01603 712362, www.swancraft.co.uk

Swan Line Cruisers Ltd   **22, 31, 39** 113
Alrewas, Trent and Mersey Canal
Tel: 01283 790332

Teddesley Boat Company   **22, 41** 114
Penkridge, Staffordshire and Worcestershire Canal
Tel: 01785 714692, www.narrowboats.co.uk

Telstar Cruisers Ltd   **9, 26, 34** 115
Tewkesbury, River Avon
Tel:01684 294088, www.telstarcruisers.co.uk

Thistle Boats   **61** 116
Linlithgow, Union Canal
Tel: 0131 621 0950, www.linnet.co.uk/tour/thistle

Topcraft Cruisers   **57** 74
Oulton Broad, River Waveney
Tel: 01502 563719

Union Canal Carriers Ltd   **31, 39, 46** 117
Braunston, Grand Union Canal
Tel: 01788 890784

Valley Cruises Ltd   **31, 39** 118
Nuneaton, Coventry Canal
Tel: 024 7639 3333, www.valleycruises.co.uk

Viking Afloat   **18, 22, 34, 41** 119
Gailey, Staffordshire and Worcestershire Canal
Tel: 01905 610660, www.viking-afloat.com

Viking Afloat   **31, 39** 120
Rugby, Oxford Canal
Tel: 01905 610660, www.viking-afloat.com

Viking Afloat   **12, 41** 121
Whitchurch, Llangollen Canal
Tel: 01905 610660, www.viking-afloat.com

Viking Afloat   **9, 26, 34** 122
Worcester, Worcester and Birmingham Canal
Tel: 01905 610660, www.viking-afloat.com

VIP Harvey Eastwood   **57** 3
Brundall, River Yare
Tel: 01603 713345, www.vip-he.demon.co.uk

Water Babies   **16** 123
Forton, Lancaster Canal
Tel: 01524 791984, www.water-babies.co.uk

Water Travel Ltd   **18, 22, 34, 41** 124
Wolverhampton, Shropshire Union Canal
Tel: 01902 782371

Welsh Lady Cruisers   **12** 85
Whittington, Llangollen Canal
Tel: 01691 662424, www.maestermyn.co.uk

Weltonfield Narrowboats Ltd   **31, 39, 46** 125
Welton, Grand Union Canal, Leicester Line
Tel: 01327 842282, www.weltonfield.co.uk

Wessex Narrowboats   **36** 87
Trowbridge, Kennet and Avon Canal
Tel: 01225 769847, www.wessexboats.co.uk

West Highland Sailing   **59** 126
Laggan, Caledonian Canal
Tel: 01809 501234

Whispering Reeds   **57** 127
Hickling, River Thurne
Tel: 01692 598314

White Horse Boats   **36** 128
Devizes, Kennet and Avon Canal
Tel: 01380 728504

Willow Wren Cruising Holidays   **31, 39** 120
Rugby, Oxford Canal
Tel: 01788 569153 / 562183, www.willowwren.co.uk

Woods Dyke Boatyard Ltd   **57** 69
Horning, River Bure
Tel: 01692 630461, www.woodsdyke-boatyard.co.uk

Wyvern Shipping Co Ltd   **45** 129
Linslade, Grand Union Canal
Tel: 01525 372355, www.canalholidays.co.uk

Booking Agents
Blakes Holiday Boating
Tel: 01603 739400, www.blakes.co.uk
Drifters Narrow Boat Holidays
Tel: 01905 721300, www.drifters.co.uk
Holidays in the UK
Tel: 01756 701199, www.holidayuk.co.uk/afloat
Hoseasons Holidays Ltd
Tel: 01502 501010, www.hoseasons.co.uk

Hotel Boats

Actief Barge Cruising Holidays
Actief on the River Thames
Tel: 01491 641237

Altken Grange Cruising Company
Tiny Purple on canals, including the north
Tel: 0114 243 0964

Caledonian Discovery
Fingal of Caledonia on the Caledonian Canal
Tel: 01397 772167

Country Hotel Narrowboats
Conwy and Caernarfon on canals and rivers
Tel: 07966 156473

Dale and Shire Hotel Narrowboats
Bittell and Earlswood on canals, including the north
Tel: 01628 603764

Duke and Duchess Hotel Narrowboats
Duke and Duchess on canals and rivers
Tel: 01908 698416

English Holiday Cruises
Oliver Cromwell and Edward Elgar on the River
Severn
Tel: 01803 328000

English Waterway Cruises
Caldon and Ashby on canals
Tel: 07973 729943

European Waterways Ltd
Scottish Highlander on the Caledonian Canal
Tel: 01784 482439

FGC Holidays
Leonora on canals
Tel: 01285 720510

H & H Narrowboat Hotels
Hind and Hart on canals
Tel: 020 7272 0033

Heads of the Valley Hotel Boats
Rose of Brecon and Abergavenny Castle on the
Monmouthshire and Brecon Canal
Tel: 01874 665315

Heart of England Hotel Narrowboats
Rose and Castle on canals
Tel: 07831 566373

Highland Steamboat Holidays Ltd
VIC32 on the Crinan and Caledonian Canals
Tel: 01546 510232

Hobo Holidays Ltd
Merganser on the River Thames
Tel: 01992 550616

Hotel Boat Boston
Boston on canals
Tel: 07889 987969

Hotel Boat Harlequin
Harlequin on the Kennet and Avon Canal and River Thames
Tel: 07703 218239

Hotel Boat Heather
Heather on canals
Tel: 01756 700144

Hotel Boat Helen of the West
Helen of the West on the Kennet and Avon Canal
Tel: 07971 599379

Inland Waterway Holiday Cruises
Snipe and Taurus on canals
Tel: 07831 110811

Loch Ness and Great Glen Cruise Co
Spirit of Loch Ness on the Caledonian Canals
Tel: 01463 711913

Narrowboat Hotel Company
Dawn and Dusk on canals
Tel: 07836 600029

Rushbrooke Narrow Boats
Brackley and Ellesmere on canals
Tel: 01926 642060

Swan and Mallard Hotelboats
Swan and Mallard on canals
Tel: 07721 679671

T & T Narrowboats
Tsarina and Tsarevna on canals
Tel: 07711 836441

Thames and Chilterns Holiday Cruises
Tranquil Rose on canals and the River Thames
Tel: 07966 248079

Thames Heritage Cruising
Dudley Thomas on the River Thames
Tel: 020 8395 0158

The River Centre
Yaffle and Ouzel on the River Avon
Tel: 07973 838526

Westover Boat Company
Barcis and Peggotty on the River Great Ouse
Tel: 01480 433768

Wood Owl Hotel Narrowboat
Wood Owl on canals
Tel: 01326 563554

Booking Agents
Hotel Boat Travel
www.canal-cruises.com

Community Boats

Community Boats Association
Hartshill Yard, Atherstone Road, Hartshill,
Nuneaton, Warwickshire, CV10 0TB.
www.communityboats.org.uk

Canoes & Camping Skiffs

Camping Skiff Holidays
Bridge Boathouses, Richmond on Thames
Tel: 020 8948 8270

The Seven Wonders

Robert Aickman, a prolific writer, was one of the energetic founders of the early campaigning charity 'The Inland Waterways Association' (still active) and compiled a list of Seven Wonders of the Waterways World in his guide book 'Know Your Waterways'. In order of date of construction, they were:-

Bingley Five Rise Locks (1774)   53
Leeds and Liverpool Canal
Five wide staircase locks rising 60 feet.
Magnificent staircase flight, an early wonder.

Burnley Embankment (1797)   50
Leeds and Liverpool Canal
3500 feet long, 40 feet above the town.
Created from the spoil from cuttings and tunnels to the north.

Pontcysyllte Aqueduct (1805)   12
Llangollen Canal
1007 feet long,126 feet above the River Dee.
Perhaps the most famous inland waterway structure.
Longest and tallest. A breathtaking experience.
Water conduit to Crewe.

Caen Hill Locks (1810-1950)   36
Kennet and Avon Canal
29 locks with side pounds rising 130 feet.
Tightly crowded locks. Below each set of bottom gates there is a huge oblong lake on the hillside that acts as a reservoir to supply the water for working the next lock down the flight. Restored 1990.

Standedge Tunnel (1811-1905)   33
Huddersfield Narrow Canal
17,094 feet long, 638 feet below Marsden Moor.
Highest above sea level (645 feet), longest and deepest below ground. Reopened Autumn 2001.

Anderton Lift (1875-1986)   29, 43
Trent and Mersey Canal / Weaver Navigation
Two tanks 75 feet long and sitting on interconnected 3 foot diameter hydraulic rams, lifted boats up 50 feet from the River Weaver to the Trent and Mersey Canal. Later converted to a counterweighted system (1908). Due to reopen 2002.

Barton Swing Aqueduct (1893)   50
Bridgewater Canal
(235 feet long swing section, 40 feet over Manchester Ship Canal)
1450 ton swinging replacement for an equally significant 'wonder' which was a tourist attraction in its time, the first stone aqueduct taking navigable water over navigable water (1761-1893).

to which Seven Wonders, I would add
Foxton Inclined Plane (1900-1911)   31
Grand Union Canal
(75 feet rise with cassions designed for wide boats) Installed before electricity. Daily standby steaming became uneconomic. There was little traffic because the Watford Locks to the south were never widened as originally intended. Closed after eleven years (1911). Derelict (2001), restoration under consideration.

and the new
Falkirk Wheel (2002)   59
Forth & Clyde Canal / Union Canal
Highly sculptural revolving boat lift connecting the two canals for the first time in ? years. First of its type in the world. New construction, 120 year design life. Due to open 2002.

Top Waterway Features

Use a tunnel or work a lock flight and you maybe wonder if there are longer versions elsewhere. Below are the top twenties:

Longest tunnels
17,094' **Standedge**, Huddersfield Narrow Canal
 9462' **Dudley**, Birmingham Canal Navigations
 9168' **Blisworth**, Grand Union Canal
 9081' **Netherton**, Birmingham Canal Navigations
 8757' **Harecastle**, Trent and Mersey Canal
 8178' **Wast Hill**, Worcester and Birmingham Canal
 6144' **Braunston**, Grand Union Canal
 4920' **Foulridge**, Leeds and Liverpool Canal
 4584' **Crick**, Grand Union Canal
 3717' **Preston Brook**, Trent and Mersey Canal
 3498' **Husbands Bosworth**, Grand Union Canal
 2880' **Islington**, Grand Union Canal
 2640' **Saddington**, Grand Union Canal
 1839' **Shortwood**, Worcester and Birmingham Canal
 1740' **Tardebigge**, Worcester and Birmingham Canal
 1716' **Barnton**, Trent and Mersey Canal
 1677' **Gannow**, Leeds and Liverpool Canal
 1671' **Gosty Hill**, Birmingham Canal Navigations

Longest lock flights
30 **Tardebigge**, Worcester and Birmingham Canal
29 **Caen Hill**, Kennet and Avon Canal
25 **Lapworth**, Stratford-upon-Avon Canal
21 **Hatton**, Grand Union Canal
21 **Wolverhampton**, Birmingham Canal Navigations
16 **Marple**, Peak Forest Canal
16 **Stourbridge**, Stourbridge Canal
15 **Audlem**, Shropshire Union Canal
14 **Deepcut**, Basingstoke Canal
13 **Perry Barr**, Birmingham Canal Navigations
13 **Farmer's Bridge**, Birmingham Canal Navigations
13 **Rothersthorpe**, Grand Union Canal
12 **Bosley**, Macclesfield Canal
11 **Tinsley**, Sheffield and South Yorkshire Canal
11 **Aston**, Birmingham Canal Navigations
 9 **Rushall**, Birmingham Canal Navigations
 9 **Napton**, Oxford Canal
 8 **Walsall**, Birmingham Canal Navigations
 8 **Ryders Green**, Birmingham Canal Navigations
 8 **Delph Nine**, Birmingham Canal Navigations

Oldest canals and navigation improvements
1566 **Exeter Ship Canal**
1639 **Avon Navigation (Warwickshire)**
1653 **Wey Navigation**
1699, 1702 **Aire and Calder Navigation**
1732 **Weaver Navigation**
1757 **Sankey Brook / St Helens Canal**
1762 **Bridgewater Canal**
1769 **Birmingham Canal Navigations**
1769 **Lee Navigation**
1770 **Calder and Hebble Navigation**
1771, 1790 **Coventry Canal**
1771 **Droitwich (Barge) Canal**
1772 **Staffordshire and Worcestershire Canal**
1774 **Huddersfield Broad Canal**
1774 **Leeds and Liverpool Canal**
1775, 1779 **Chester Canal**
1777 **Chesterfield Canal**
1778 **Erewash Canal**
1778 **Loughborough Navigation**
1778, 1790 **Oxford Canal**

This book is dedicated to
Annabelle
with us on many cruises.

I also thank Jackie, my wife and companion on over 2300 miles of waterway travel, and my waterway friends who have been supportive throughout this project.

Thanks must also go to the production team at GEOprojects (UK) Ltd:

Mary Spence General Manager, Caleb Gould Cartographic Assistant, David Edwards Cartographic Draughtsman, Ian Brown Cartographic Draughtsman

Special thanks to Graham Fisher MBE for his help and advice on aspects of particular waterways covered in this book.

I asked Jackie to suggest villages that have been 'well worth the walk'. Memories of country villages tend to merge into one idealistic image, many experiences contributing to that rosy glow. Her top twenty, chosen from lots of candidates, are: **Audlem** Shropshire Union Canal, **Braunston** Oxford Canal, **Brewood** Shropshire Union Canal, **Brinklow** Oxford Canal, **Burston** (a hamlet) Trent and Mersey Canal, **Dorchester** River Thames, **Gargrave** Leeds and Liverpool Canal, **Great Bedwyn** Kennet and Avon Canal, **Kintbury** Kennet and Avon Canal, **Lower Heyford** Oxford Canal, **Lymm** Bridgewater Canal, **Marple** Peak Forest and Macclesfield Canals, **Saltaire** Leeds and Liverpool Canal, **Shardlow** Trent and Mersey Canal, **Skipton** Leeds and Liverpool Canal, **South Stoke** River Thames, **Stoke Breune** Grand Union Canal, **Sutton Cheyney** Ashby Canal, **Tewkesbury** River Avon, **Whaley Bridge** Peak Forest Canal.

This book has taken some months in preparation. If you find corrections are needed please let me know. In any event, I hope that you will take advantage of our waterways and enjoy them as much as we do. *brian-roberts@britains-waterways.com*

If you wish to dip further into the world of waterways, there are 3 magazines to read:
Canal Boat & Inland Waterways Tel: 0118 977 1677 www.systemD.net/canalboat
Canal & Riverboat Tel: 01372 741441 www. canalriverboat.enta.net
Waterways World Tel: 01283 742970

The following websites may prove useful when planning your holidays:
Holiday site www.waterwayholidaysuk.com
From the British Tourist Authority www.visitbritain.com/activities/waterways
Introductions for overseas visitors www.canaljunction.com and www.canalia.com
Britain Express - an internet magazine for anglophiles www.britainexpress.com
Inland Waterways Association: campaigning charity www.waterways.org.uk
British Waterways: official site www.britishwaterways.co.uk
Environment Agency: keeper of rivers and fens www.environment-agency.gov.uk
George's: an enthusiasts' much respected site www.canals.com
New listing of waterways interests www.waterwaysdirectory.com
Opinions and news www.narrowboatworld.com
Waterway museums www.nwm.org.uk, www.canaljunction.com/mussbcn/htm, wwwboatmuseum.org.uk and www.canalmuseum.org.uk
Notes on safe and friendly cruising www.ownerships.co.uk/saftey.htm
To work out detailed travel times www.canalplan.org.uk
For cruising maps of the waterways www.geoprojects-maps.co.uk

Photographs in this book supplied by kind permission:
© Harry Arnold - pp 8 *left*, 14, 15 *top*, 23 *bottom*, 28 *bottom*, 35 *bottom*, 51 *bottom*, 53, 57
© Alan Barnes - pp 10, 11, 21 *bottom*, 38 *top*, 47 *top*, cover *top right*
© Bath Tourism Bureau - p 36
© Don Bellham - pp 12, 25 *bottom*, 30 *top*, 42, cover *bottom left*
© British Waterways - p 61
© Graham Fisher MBE - pp 19 *bottom*, 23 *top*, 35 *top*, 38 *bottom*
© Terry Griffths - p 17
© Guildford Borough Council - p 24
© Llangollen International Musical Eisteddfod - p 13 *bottom*
© Kevin Maslin - pp 13 *top*, 15 *bottom*, 19 *top*, 21 *top*
© Ian Meredith - pp 2, 4, 7, 9, 30 *bottom*, 32, 44 *top*, 44 *bottom*, 47 *bottom*, 52
© Brian Roberts - pp 51 *top*
© Paul Roberts - front cover flap
© Robin Smithett - pp 5, 8 *right*, 16, 25 *top*, 28 *top*, 33, 37, 40, 43, 54, 55, 56, 58, 59, 60, cover *bottom right*, cover *centre right*, cover *top left*
© Lawrence Tetley - contents page

Index of Waterways